We Confess
THE SACRAMENTS

We Confess

THE SACRAMENTS

We Confess Series, Volume 2

Hermann Sasse

Translated by Norman Nagel

Publishing House
St. Louis

Copyright © 1985 Concordia Publishing House
3558 South Jefferson Avenue, St. Louis, MO 63118-3968
Manufactured in the United States of America

Library of Congress Cataloging in Publication Data
(Revised for volume 2)

Sasse, Hermann, 1895-
    We confess.

    Translation of selected essays from: In statu confessionis.
    Contents: v. 1. Jesus Christ—v. 2. The sacraments.
    1. Theology—Addresses, essays, lectures. 2. Lutheran Church—Doctrines—Addresses, essays, lectures.   I. Title.
BR85.S21613   1984   230'.41   84-7043
ISBN 0-570-03941-X (v. 1 : pbk.)
ISBN 0-570-03982-7 (v. 2)

---

1 2 3 4 5 6 7 8 9 10   PP   94 93 92 91 90 89 88 87 86 85

Contents

Translator's Preface

Hermann Sasse's confession of Jesus Christ we have heard in volume one of the We Confess Series, *We Confess Jesus Christ*. In this volume he confesses that the salvation achieved by Christ alone is ours by His gift alone. His ways of giving are His to determine as He pleases. Only thus are they sure and liberating in their bestowal of what He says He is giving. We may in no way make His means of grace subject to our determinations. His are the words we are given to proclaim; His is the name put on us with the water of Baptism; His is the body and blood, which He gives into our mouths to eat and to drink; His is the forgiveness bestowed with the words of absolution; His are the keys entrusted to His ministry. All this Sasse confesses against every attempt to take them captive.

He speaks with powerful contemporary relevance because he knows the historical challenges. From its beginning the Gospel has suffered subversion, dilution, and addition. Men have attempted to make it more sure and more acceptable. Knowledge of these attempts is a resource for dealing with them, and Sasse recalls it for us as he points to Christ.

More than a defender of the faith, Sasse is at his happiest and best extolling his Lord. Jesus is the Lord. His salvation is ours only as His gift, and He gives it according to His good and gracious will. No necessity may be laid on Him in the ways of Scholastic or Enlightenment theology. Sasse's enormous learning and careful scholarship are put to this service.

He was so engaged in addressing the heavy needs of the day that his work comes to us mostly as a series of particular pieces, each with its own weight. The first of these essays, "Word and Sacrament: Preaching and the Lord's Supper," describes the life of the church as it moves forward from generation to generation. Its continuity is given only by the Lord and the continuity of His gifts. The church is where He gives His gifts, where the means of grace are made available. Only by them

9

is it enlivened, sustained, and given a foretaste of the consummation to come. This first essay ends with a cry to the Holy Spirit: *Veni creator Spiritus.*

In 1949 Sasse wrote "Holy Baptism" in response to Barth's attack on Baptism. The progression of the essay is most instructive. First comes the contemporary church context, then history, theology, and Scripture. There is often a generating and focusing *Leitmotif* in Sasse's writings, and in this essay it is "Washing of Regeneration."

Sasse's primary study and training in the New Testament are witnessed in his thoroughgoing exegesis in "The Lord's Supper in the New Testament." Our Lord's life-giving Supper flows into the church, making it His body. Sasse extols the body and blood given and shed for us Christians to eat and to drink. Thereby we are enlivened for worship and work.

The vitality of these gifts is then confessed in "The Lord's Supper in the Lutheran Church." What is said of it in the Augsburg Confession is prompting for rejoicing and repentance. Again Sasse relates the discussion to the contemporary situation, history, theology, and Scripture. What our Lord says, does, and gives affects our lives, confession, and work.

What our Lord says and does is extolled in "The Lutheran Understanding of the Consecration." This may not be blurred or diminished by Protestant influences, Anglican ornamentation, or Roman infiltration. The enlivening gifts given by our Lord and confessed by our fathers direct our understanding, for we are captive to the Word.

The final essay, "Sanctorum Communio," points us toward the next volume, *We Confess the Church.* Sasse's understanding is rooted in his own profound ecumenical involvement. To forsake the doctrine of the Real Presence of the body and blood of Christ is to forsake the catholic tradition and what our Lord says. To be given His body and blood to eat and to drink is to be part of His body, the *una sancta,* which continues forever and is thus brought to the consummation. The faith that confesses this is not grounded in our observations or ideas but in the words of our Lord. Confessing His sacraments, we confess also His church.

WORD AND SACRAMENT
Preaching
and the Lord's Supper

Letters to Lutheran Pastors, No. 42
July 1956

(Published in *In Statu Confessionis: Gesammelte Aufsätze von Hermann Sasse*, ed. Friedrich Wilhelm Hopf [Berlin and Hamburg: Lutherisches Verlagshaus, 1966], 73–90.)

There is probably no question that leads so deeply into our office, its essence and its task, its necessity and its promise, as our present subject. Whenever theology becomes quite practical, it engages this problem. The profoundest Christian thinkers have pondered it, and it has affected all the churches of the world, the "Catholic" no less than the "Protestant." It is a problem not only for Protestantism, or for Lutheranism in particular. The Catholic churches of the East and West also have their problems with preaching and the Lord's Supper. The Eastern Orthodox Church, for example, which has gained a firm foothold in the West because of the massive migration of Orthodox Christians from Eastern countries, cannot be satisfied with continuing to celebrate its "Holy Liturgy" in the liturgical languages when it is no longer understood by the younger generation. They have to make use of their principle that the liturgy be celebrated in the language of the people. So an English translation has already been completed. But the liturgy must also be explained. Can the Eastern Church ever forget that its greatest preacher was John Chrysostom and that it is not enough to venerate his icon—that his example must also be followed?

Similar questions arise for Roman Catholicism, as the liturgical movement indicates. It was born before the First World War out of a deep dissatisfaction on the part of the best young Catholics with the situation in their church. After 1918 it pointed out the shortcomings of the common Catholic worship so candidly that it had to be curbed and in part shut down by Rome. But the Curia had absorbed its great desire to elevate the major European languages to the position of liturgical languages with such vigor that we can still expect a major reform of the Roman liturgy in this century.

Is it a coincidence that the liturgical movement in Germany and other countries went hand in hand with a "Bible movement" and that the modern Roman church has produced masterpieces of Biblical translation? Is it a coincidence that the Roman church in the age of radio and television has again produced popular preaching that recalls the classical period of popular preaching in the Middle Ages?

But the encouragement of Bible reading and the special popular preaching are no substitute for the every Sunday parish sermon, especially if the latter is only a short lecture on a question of dogmatics or ethics. Truly, the problem of "Word and Sacrament: Preaching and the Lord's Supper" is not only our problem but that of all Christendom. Strictly speaking, it has been a problem throughout the history of the church, ever since Paul had to deal with the problems of the Lord's Supper (1 Cor. 10 and 11) and preaching (1 Cor. 14) in the church at Corinth.

1.

Old as the problem of Word and Sacrament is, it was first put as a theological question and given a theological answer by Augustine. Here, as in other matters, this great church father of the West is not always helpful, and we may not follow him as blindly as did the theology not only of the Catholicism of the Middle Ages but also of the Reformation. This can even be said of Luther himself, although he was able to break through the constructions of Augustine's sacramental doctrine at decisive points by bringing to light the witness of Scripture, a witness that was better maintained by the Eastern fathers. Since we have been reared in Augustine's sacramental teaching and even see Luther's teaching on the Sacrament through Augustinian spectacles, it is not easy. But should we just leave it to Roman Catholic theologians to recover something of the rich resources of the Greek fathers, who have such a great role to play in the Catalog of Testimonies at the conclusion of the

Formula of Concord (*Die Bekenntnisschriften der evangelisch-luther-ischen Kirche*, 6th ed. [Göttingen, 1967], 1101–35) as witnesses of Scriptural truth, just as they frequently appear also in the earlier Confessions?

Wherein lies the weakness of Augustine's sacramental doctrine? This may first of all be found in his attempt to establish *sacramentum* as a universal idea or category that applies to all religions [*Con. Faustum* 19. 11]. The Christian sacrament is then only a specific instance of a universal phenomenon common to all religions, both the true and the false. Now it is true that the Christian sacraments, such as Baptism and the Lord's Supper, have their parallels in many religions, as the apologists of the second century, and even Paul in 1 Cor. 10:18–21, have observed. No one denies that heathen rites and the myths they follow have echoes of the original knowledge of God, but through sin they have been perverted into the service of idols [Rom. 1:19–23]. In this sense, even the human sacrifices of the Teutons, the Aztecs, and the Syrians could be regarded as demonically perverted hints pointing to the sacrifice of the Son of Man. "Every dogma is as old as the world."

But to try to understand the Christian sacrament on the basis of a concept of sacrament derived from the history of religions is totally impossible. What constitutes the church's sacrament is something unique; it has no parallels. All the honor and love we owe Augustine as a great father of the Western Church may not obscure the fact that he had lived too long and too deeply in heathen religion and philosophy. He was not able to banish the old man from his thinking in the same way that he was from his life and faith. That is what it cost him to have "loved so late."

We may find something similar in what Augustine taught on Holy Scripture. Here also he has a universal idea or category of what "divine scripture" is and must be. This he applies to the Bible and shows how it matches his ideal instead of simply starting with what Holy Scripture has to say about itself. Had he done this, he would not have been able to put the Sibylline Oracles on a level with the prophets because they apparently correctly prophesied the coming of the Redeemer [*De. civ.* 18. 23]. As the Bible is not just a specific instance of what may be called "divine scripture" in the religions of the world, so also the Christian sacrament cannot be understood from a universal idea of *sacramentum*. The Christian sacrament is what it is because it was instituted by Jesus Christ and so is inextricably bound up with the incarnation of the eternal Son of God.

The theological tradition of the West has shown a remarkable stability through the Middle Ages into modern Catholicism. The same may be said of Lutheran and Reformed theology in the Reformation and through the period of orthodoxy. In doing theology, we simply may not spare ourselves the labor of differentiating between what the Bible says and the human mode of thinking. This is so even for so central a doctrine of the Christian faith as the doctrine of the Trinity. With the East one can think of it as three in one [*Dreieinigkeit*], with Augustine and the West as threefold [*Dreifaltigkeit*], without in any way diminishing the truth of the impenetrable mystery.

It was one of the mistakes of our fathers in the age of orthodoxy that they all too often identified the thought form with the Biblical content of a doctrinal statement. As a result they unconsciously and unintentionally clothed the eternal truth of Scripture in the transitory garb of a theological tradition. It should not be necessary to point out that this observation has nothing to do with the attempt of the Ritschlian School, above all of Harnack in his *History of Dogma*, to rob Christian dogma of its Biblical content by replacing what were taken to be the categories of Greek metaphysics with those of Kantian ethics. Nor does it have anything to do with the modern "demythologizing" of the New Testament by translating the Biblical statements into existential philosophy. What we have in mind here is what Luther did when he confronted the falsification of the Biblical faith by Aristotelian and Thomistic philosophy and when he told the Swiss, who so energetically appealed to Augustinian metaphysics in the Marburg Colloquy, where the limit of the authority of the church fathers is:

> We would indeed show the beloved fathers such honor that we read what they have written, which is so helpful to us, with the best understanding of which we are capable, insofar as they are in harmony with Holy Scripture. But where their writings are not in harmony with Holy Scripture, it is much better that we say they are mistaken than that because of them we depart from God's Word. (According to Osiander's report, which is confirmed by the reports of others, that Luther appealed to Augustine's own rule, according to which only the canonical books of Scripture have unqualified authority; see the texts, WA 30/III, 144–45, and W. Koehler, *Das Marburger Religionsgespräch: Versuch einer Rekonstruktion*, where several sources are cited on p. 177.)

It would have been better for the Lutheran Church if its theologians had always held to this rule in more rigorous self-criticism.

The practical consequence of the foregoing is that we must claim our freedom from the Augustinian school's universal idea of the *sacramentum*, as our Confessions essentially do when they do not first set down a definition of the nature of a sacrament and even leave the question of the number of sacraments open, in contrast with Rome (not more and not less than seven) and the Reformed Church (not more and not less than two). The way of the Confessions is in harmony with teaching of the early church, which was innocent of any such idea of sacrament. They spoke of particular "mysteries," using the word *mystery* quite broadly. In the 11th century the Latin *sacramentum* was still being used so broadly that Hugh of St. Victor, besides his other dogmatic works, wrote a dogmatics with the title *De sacramentis*, in which even the Trinity is called a *sacramentum*, that is, a mystery, something known only to faith. The classical dogmatician of the Eastern Church, John of Damascus, also knows no doctrine of the sacraments as such. He has chapters on "The Faith and Baptism" and on "The Holy Spotless Mysteries of the Lord," that is, the Eucharist [*De Fide* 4. 9. 13]. In harmony with this, when Luther uses the word *Sacrament* in the singular, he usually means "the Sacrament of sacraments," as the Sacrament of the Altar was first called by the fathers of the Greek church. There is an echo of this Lutheran usage in Justus Jonas's German text of the Apology when he renders Melanchthon's *eadem sacramenta* as "the same Baptism and Sacrament" (Ap VII/VIII 10). In this way also the Lutheran Church retained the freedom to call absolution a sacrament. Whether the office of the keys is called a sacrament or not is purely a matter of terminology, in which the church has and must have complete freedom if it wants to remain on the foundation of Scripture. Christ did not institute some abstract *sacramentum*. He instituted the office of the ministry, Baptism, Holy Communion, and the office of the keys. Only if we regain this freedom of the Lutheran Reformation will we be able to go all the way to the heart of what is uniquely referred to by the term "sacrament," whose essence is not to be found in any phenomena from the history of religions or in any human speculation about what God must do to redeem us. It is in the institution of the Lord that eludes every human why and in the incomprehensible wonder of the Incarnation. If we take that seriously, then the problem of Word and Sacrament takes on a completely different appearance.

2.

Augustine has left behind another difficult question for all the churches of the West in his definition of a sacrament as the "sign" [*sig-*

num] of a divine "thing" [res]. [Signacula quidem rerum divinarum esse: visibilia, sed res ipsas invisibiles in eis (De Cat. Rud. 26. 50. Con. Faustum 19. 11) Ista, fratres, ideo dicuntur sacramenta, quia in eis aliud videtur, aliud intelligitur (Serm. 272. Ep. 138. 17). Aliud est sacramentum, aliud virtus sacramenti (In Joh. Tract. 26. 11).] What we have here must first be recognized as a man's theological theory. It is quite noteworthy that the Eastern Church, which here, as always, represents an older form of Christianity, developed no such theory of sacrament as a sign of something divine. In the late Middle Ages and the century of the Reformation (Cyril Lucarius and his Calvinism) the Latin Scholastic doctrine, and with it the doctrine of sacrament as sign, did gain some entry into Eastern theology, but this private teaching today enjoys hardly any recognition, least of all by the Russian theologians. To be sure the sacraments (mysteries) are spoken of as symbols, as "the outward means of the unfathomable, hiddenly laden working of grace by the Holy Spirit through which the sanctification of man is again brought to completion" (Stef. Zankov, Das Orthodoxe Christentum [1928], 102 [The Eastern Orthodox Church (1929), 113]). What is characteristic however, is that even Dionysius the Areopagite sees what is termed sign and symbol more in the details of the celebration of the sacrament, the particular rites and ceremonies, the gestures and actions of the priest than in the sacraments as such. That is also to be understood when he speaks of the Eucharist in the plural: "the mysteries."

Thomas understands Augustine's definition of sacrament as a sign in such a way that it is spoken of as an effective sign (signum efficax). This is applied only to sacraments in the New Testament; the "sacraments" of the Old Testament have only a significative meaning. In the Eastern Church what is central is what they do. God works on man in a sacrament. "A Mystery or Sacrament is a holy act through which grace, or, in other words, the saving power of God, works mysteriously upon man." So Philaret in the Christian Catechism [284]. In such a doctrine of sacrament it can never come to that tearing apart of "sign" and "thing," signum and res that since Berengar, Wycliffe, the radical Hussites, the Devotio Moderna in the Netherlands, the Humanists, Zwingli, and Calvin has reduced sacrament to being only a sign of grace. This is probably not what Augustine had in mind. There are two levels in his sacramental doctrine—one, as presented in the liturgy, catholic realistic, the other spiritualizing. This split is the tribute he pays to Neoplatonic philosophy and is a burden that the churches in the West bear to this day. We in no way want to glorify the teaching of the Eastern Church

16

here or excuse its serious errors, but on this one point it stands nearer to the New Testament than what Augustine and those who followed him taught. *The New Testament does not know of the idea of sacrament as sign.* Perhaps the whole idea of sign originated in the designation of circumcision as a "sign of the covenant" [*signum foederis*] (Gen. 17:11). But despite the parallel drawn in Col. 1:11ff. between Baptism and circumcision—Paul was addressing Gnostics with a Jewish background—no one has ever found a place in the New Testament in which Baptism or the Lord's Supper or even the "elements" of water, bread, and wine are understood in the sense of the "sign" theory. None of the words that could be interpreted as such a "sign," such as *eikōn* (image), are used of Baptism or the Lord's Supper in the New Testament. Nowhere is it written that Baptism is an image or a sign of regeneration. It *is* the washing of regeneration (Titus 3:5). "We *were* buried therefore with Him by Baptism into death" (Rom. 6:4). "You *were* buried with Him in Baptism, in which you *were* also raised. . . . And you . . . God *made* alive together with Him" (Col. 2:12–13). Also the word *tupos* in the sense of model or image is not used of Baptism and the Lord's Supper or of their elements. There are "types" of the sacraments in the Old Testament, as when Paul in 1 Cor. 10:1ff., where we find Baptism and the Lord's Supper arranged together for the first time in the New Testament (cf. 12:13; John 19:34), points to certain experiences of the old people of God as "typological" [*tupikōs*] (1 Cor. 10:11, which the Vulgate accurately translates *in figura* [Tertullian, *figurate, Idol.* 5]) of the sacraments of the new people of God. So the "baptism" of the fathers in the cloud and in the sea, the "spiritual food" of the manna, the bread from heaven (cf John 6:31ff.), and the "spiritual drink" of the water from the rock are types, prefigurements of Christian Baptism and the Lord's Supper. But Baptism and the Lord's Supper are not "types," not prefigurements or parables. They do indeed point to the future, but it is a future already present with its gifts of grace. More will be said later on what it means that the future is present in the sacraments.

Here is where we find the heart of the Lutheran confession of the sacraments. Certainly Luther made much use, especially in his early period, of Augustine's idea of sacrament as a "sign." Here as in other patterns of theological thought he was bound by the theological schooling from which he came. We should not overlook the fact that until 1522 he had to carry on the struggle against Rome for the *sola fide* also in regard to sacrament according to the old formula: *Non sacramentum, sed fides sacramenti justificat* (Not the sacrament, but the faith of the one receiving the sacrament justifies). To that Luther always clung, with special emphasis at the point where he had to join the "through faith alone" in Baptism with the objectivity of the sacrament. "My faith does not constitute Baptism but receives it." This is from the Large Catechism, where Luther is defending the Baptism of infants (LC IV 53); it is sure for them, too. If the unqualified adherence to the *sola fide* is one side of the sacramental teaching of Luther and the Lutheran Church, the other is the insistence on the objectivity and reality of the sacrament, which was necessary over against the Enthusiasts. How serious this was for Luther is shown by the fact that he went beyond Thomas in his insistence on objectivity. Thomas stated, "An adult who lacked the intention [*intentio*] of receiving baptism should be rebaptized [*esset rebaptizandus*]," in order to receive Baptism validly and without question. But if the lack of intention is not certain, in case of doubt it should be conditional (*Summa theol.* 3. 68. 7. 3). Luther regarded the baptism of a Jew, who "should come today deceitfully and with an evil purpose," as a true baptism (LC IV 54), which under no circumstances is it to be repeated if the sinner should come to faith. This objectivity of the sacrament was settled for the Reformer from the very beginning, just as he always held fast to the Real Presence, even when he finally gave up transubstantiation in *The Babylonian Captivity*.

But the more he had to urge the objectivity of the sacrament against the "Sacramentarians," the more cautious he became in using the word *sign*. They were misusing it in a way that made of sacrament only a sign. In the Catechism he avoids the word *sign*, and we need only look at the Heidelberg Catechism to understand what that means. Here the sacraments (Question 66) are understood only as "signs and seals" [*Wahrzeichen und Siegel*] and no other effect is ascribed to them than of reminding believers of the actual salvation event and assuring them of it. This actual event is independent of the sacrament. Question 72 asks, "Is the outward washing with water itself actually the washing away of sins?" to which the answer is given: "No, for only the blood of Jesus Christ and the Holy Spirit cleanse us from all sin." The following question, why the Holy Spirit calls Baptism the washing of regeneration and the washing away of sins, is given the answer that He wants to teach us "that *just as* the filthiness of the body is taken away, so are our sins taken away by the blood and Spirit of Christ" and "that He wants to assure us through this divine *pledge* and *sign* [*Pfand und Wahrzeichen*] that we just as truly have been washed of our sins spiritually as we are washed with physical water." In the Lord's Supper

18

bread and cup are *"signs [Wahrzeichen] of the body and blood of Christ"* (Q. 75). Only "according to the nature and usage of sacraments" is the bread called the body of Christ (Q. 78). The bread *is not* the body, and so the body and blood of the Lord are not taken orally (Q. 76 and 77).

Under the pressure of such spiritualizing Luther more and more stepped back from the conventional word *sign* and also *pledge* [*pignus*], which was much beloved in the theology of the Middle Ages and had meant much to him in his early years. He was profoundly aware that sacrament has another side, the "external thing," which the Enthusiasts scorned (LC IV 7), the "gross, external mask," i. e., outward form [*Erscheinungsform*] (LC IV 19). However, as it is of the nature of divine revelation that God comes to us veiled, as the Incarnate One ("In our poor flesh and blood, Enclothes himself the eternal Good"), so is it of the nature of divine action "that God will not deal with us except through his external Word and sacrament" (SA III VIII 10). In this recognition of the indissoluble unity of "sign" and "object" [*Zeichen und Sache*] the danger of spiritualizing is overcome—the danger that lay in what Augustine taught and that since Berengar and Wycliffe captured so many Catholics of the late Middle Ages and since Zwingli and Bucer a large part of the Reformation movement. In this sense what Luther taught on sacraments is the great overthrow of Augustinianism in the church and the return to the essence [*Est*] of the New Testament.

3.

The third problem, which Augustine never fully found his way through, is the question of "Word" and "element." He first of all gave the solution that is quoted again and again in the Middle Ages, in modern Roman theology, and by the reformers: "Take the Word away, and what is the water but simply water? The Word is added to the element, and there results a sacrament, as if itself also a kind of visible Word" (*In Joh. Tract.* 80. 3). Of first importance here is the emphasis on the Word as that which constitutes the sacrament. It was a serious error to try to explain sacrament from the natural side [*Naturseite*], as was done in the 19th century under the influence of theosophical speculations, which even infiltrated Lutheran theology, and in the 20th century in the Berneuchener Movement influenced by Rudolf Steiner. The most impressive attempt to understand sacrament from nature was made by Paul Tillich in his early writings and in his dogmatics. He presents the view that in a sacrament an element from nature becomes the "bearer of the holy" [*Symbol und Wirklichkeit* (1966), 50; *Systematic Theology* (1963), 3:123]. That is supposed to be the essence of the Lutheran idea of sacrament. It is significant that Catholic theology must be brought to bear against him. It is not some mysterious quality of the water in Baptism or the bread and wine in the Lord's Supper but only the institution of the Lord that has designated just these elements, and His almighty Word alone makes them sacraments. Later as Scholasticism spoke of "Word" and "element" as "form" and "substance" and this was taken into Roman dogma, the constituting significance of the Word for a sacrament was underscored because the "form," the "idea," is always regarded as higher than the "substance." We should never forget that nor misunderstand it, as though the sacramental word in the Catholic sacrament is a kind of incantation with a magical effect, as Protestant polemic has often understood it. Johann Gerhard (Locus 21, 13) emphatically repudiates the Reformed understanding of the Roman and Lutheran consecration as a magical incantation [*magica incantatio*]. There may be a suggestion of "magic" in the Roman view that at ordination a power to consecrate [*potestas consecrandi*] is given to particular men as a *virtus*, a power in them. But even we would not acknowledge that, because today "magic" is generally understood as exercising coercion over the deity. In any case we must grant that the Roman Church also puts the Word above the element. What then is the relation of Word to element? What may be said of the element in the sacrament?

The answer that emerges may at first surprise us. The "element" does not at all belong to the essence of "sacrament." This follows from the fact that the medieval church had to abandon the idea of element and replace it with "substance" [*Materie*], which does not have to be an element, a thing of nature [*Naturding*] at all. So in the Sacrament of Penance what was done by the penitent (contrition, confession, satisfaction) was understood as the substance, while the absolution was its form. (Time will not allow us here to explore the magnificent attempt of Hugo of St. Victor, the first dogmatician of the medieval church, to construct a doctrine of the sacraments without the apparatus of Aristotelian philosophy. In spite of his beginning with Augustine's definition of sacrament as the "sign" of a holy "thing," he tries to keep clear of any philosophical system; *De Sacramentis* 1. 9.) Also the Augsburg Confession and its Apology do not know the idea of element with sacrament as such. This is shown by the inclusion of absolution among the sacraments (AC XIII): "The genuine sacraments, therefore, are Bap-

tism, the Lord's Supper, and absolution" (Ap XIII 4). In Gospel freedom
the Apology (Ap XIII 11) declares that even ordination may be called
a sacrament because Christ has instituted the office of the ministry and
given it the promise of Is. 55:11. This freedom in speaking of sacraments
in the Lutheran Church includes the freedom to regard the formula
"Word and element" as what it is, a theological attempt to describe
sacrament. The concept of *elementum* is dubious because of its ambiguity (consider the manifold meaning of the word in the New Testament)
and vagueness, and we might well ask whether the reformers have done
well in taking it over from Augustine's sacramental doctrine without
more reflection.

4.

What is *our task* in view of this state of affairs? As Lutheran theologians we should follow the example of the Augsburg Confession in
our theological thinking as in our teaching and preaching and never start
from one common doctrine of the means of grace or the sacraments but
deal with each of the means of grace by itself in its own particularity:
Preaching the Gospel, Baptism, confession and absolution, the Sacrament of the Altar. Only then will we be able to understand the fullness
of God's dealing with us, the different ways by which He comes to us,
and the whole uniqueness of every single means of grace and so come
to the proper use of each (consider the order of the articles of the Augsburg Confession and the arrangement of confession between Baptism
and the Lord's Supper in the Small Catechism). Already with Baptism
and the Lord's Supper it only causes confusion if we always try to draw
parallels between them and to assert that what is true of the one sacrament must be said of the other. So it has been argued recently in the
ecumenical movement even by Lutherans: Since the churches recognize
one another's Baptism, they must also have reciprocal recognition of the
Lord's Supper. As they put it, "altar fellowship" follows of necessity
from "baptismal fellowship." But Baptism and the Lord's Supper, as
immeasurably great as each of these sacraments is and as much as they
cohere (1 Cor. 10:1ff.; cf. also the baptismal practice of the early church
on Easter Eve and even the custom of the medieval church of giving
infants the Lord's Supper, at least in the form of consecrated wine, right
after baptism), are simply not the same.

What the Sacrament of the Altar is was told to us by the Lord
Himself; what Baptism is we learn from His apostle. We know when

the Lord's Supper was instituted from the account of the institution. The *institution* of Baptism, according to the common notion of the early church, and also of Luther ("To Jordan came the Christ, our Lord"), took place as a result of the Lord's letting Himself be baptized by John ("There He established a washing for us") and is not identical with the *command* to baptize. Baptism was performed in the apostolic age "in the name of Jesus" (e.g., Acts 2:38; 10:48; 19:5; cf. the command to baptize of Matt. 28:19 according to Eusebius in the apparatus of Nestle; 1 Cor. 1:13), later with the Trinitarian baptismal formula. The apostles often left the administration of baptism to others, and it is no devaluation of the sacrament for Paul to say that the Lord did not send him to baptize but to preach the Gospel. Baptism remains, with all the freedom and diversity of administration, the washing of regeneration, the full, complete sacrament, needing no completion in confirmation, as Anglican theology today says, not without effect on the Protestant churches.

We cannot go into the question here of what we would have to say today in our individual congregations about Baptism. It seems to me that the so urgently necessary instruction about the sacrament in Bible classes and sermons on the great texts of the New Testament that deal with Baptism should be taking place. Beyond that the fourth chief part of the Large Catechism should be treated in lectures and discussions. That applies especially to the question of infant baptism. We have to be aware of how ignorant the modern generation is, even in the Lutheran Church. We recognize far too seldom that religious and confirmation instruction and the Sunday school can in no way give what previous generations knew from home through Bible reading and what was learned from pious parents. Today the need of the hour for the Lutheran Church is to become a teaching church again. The success of Rome, of the sects, and of communism is based substantially on the fact that what they teach, they teach unflaggingly. And our congregations hunger more than we know for teaching. Why don't we give them the bread that they want? How often we have given the impression at the administration of baptism in the congregation or with a small baptismal party that an *opus operatus* has been administered. Who of those present knows what a miracle has happened here under the insignificant veil of the external sacrament? Who is aware that here a decision is made between the life and death, salvation and damnation of a person because this sacrament reaches into eternity? Are our congregations aware that they must pray in all seriousness for the newly baptized? Luther maintained that so many of the baptized are lost because this intercession has been lacking

(WA 19, 537f.; *Bekenntnisschriften*, "Taufbüchlein," 536, 20ff.). If this intercession were taken seriously, would it not also mean the beginning of a renewal of the office of sponsor that has become so secularized? Do we really believe that the members of our congregations take so much with them from a few hurried hours of confirmation instruction, in which something is said at the end about the sacraments—though they should really determine the whole content of confirmation instruction—that they are able to live on it throughout their whole lives as people who daily return to their baptism?

5.

Where Baptism is rightly taught, there the Gospel is rightly proclaimed, for the whole Gospel is contained in this sacrament: Christ's death and resurrection, our dying and rising with Him in repentance and faith, the bestowal already now of future heavenly treasures, eternal righteousness, innocence and blessedness. The same applies to the Sacrament of the Altar. Of it Luther once said: "This sacrament is the Gospel" ("Concerning the Veneration of the Sacrament of the Holy Body of Christ," 1523, directed to the Christians in Bohemia with a powerful emphasis on the Real Presence against every symbolic explanation). This is one of the Reformer's profoundest theological perceptions. Because this sacrament is the Gospel, the struggle over the sacrament was at the same time the struggle for the Gospel, and vice versa. That alone can explain what the world calls Luther's stubbornness and obstinacy in the controversy over the Sacrament, his inflexible seriousness on just this question. Neither for Zwingli nor for Bucer was the struggle for the Sacrament so important.

Why is the Sacrament of the Altar the Gospel for Luther? First of all simply because the Words of Institution contain the whole Gospel. To attack them is to attack the Gospel itself.

> Everything depends on these words. Every Christian should and must know them and hold them fast. He must never let anyone take them away from him by any other kind of teaching, even though it were an angel from heaven [Gal. 1:8]. They are words of life and of salvation, so that whoever believes in them has all his sins forgiven through that faith; he is a child of life and has overcome death and hell. Language cannot express how great and mighty these words are, for they are the sum and substance of the whole gospel. (WA 11, 432, 19 [American Edition 36:277])

It must be called an attack on these words if part of them is taken literally and another part figuratively, as when "Take and eat" and "Drink of it, all of you" are taken literally, "This is My body" and "This is My blood" figuratively, and then "which is given for you" and "which is shed for you" literally again. It is characteristic of Luther that right in the cited passage, as usual, he regards faith in the "for you" as most essential. It is what brings the blessing of the Sacrament. At the same time he stresses that this "for you" is inseparably bound with faith that the words "This is My body" and "This is My blood" are true and must be taken as they stand.

> Now beware of such a view. Let go of reason and intellect; for they strive in vain to understand how flesh and blood can be present, and because they do not grasp it they refuse to believe it. (WA 11, 434, 17 [American Edition 36:279])

With this understanding of the Sacrament the relationship between Word and sacrament is no longer a problem. They go together. The sacrament is the *verbum visibile* (visible Word); the Word is the *sacramentum audibile*, the audible and heard sacrament. The spoken and heard Word of itself is a thing of nature, sound waves that come from the voice box and are received by the ear. And yet we hear "in, with, and under" these sound waves, the Word of the eternal God Himself. The natural word becomes the Word of God, *is* the Word of God.

The Gospel comes to us in this twofold way, as Word and as sacrament. Thus absolution can also be counted among the sacraments: "Do you also believe that my forgiveness is God's forgiveness?" [the confessor asks]. As Christ's body and blood are hidden under the forms of bread and wine, so God's Word is hidden under the form of the human voice (and also Holy Scripture under the form of human writings). What the Word means for the Sacrament of the Altar becomes clear from the fact that nothing made such a profound impact on those who came from the Roman to the Lutheran Mass as the Words of Institution, which the German people had never heard before because they were spoken softly in the Roman Mass. Now they were chanted aloud at the altar in their own mother tongue. "Word" and "element" became one. In both God comes to us to give us *one* grace in different forms. This is surely the way of divine revelation. God does not come to us as *Deus nudus*, as Luther says, not naked, but always veiled. Thus in Christ divinity was veiled under His humanity and could only be recognized with the eyes of faith. This is the mystery of the Incarnation, in which the sacraments are rooted: "And the Word became *flesh* and dwelt among us, full of grace and truth; *we* have beheld His glory." "We," that is, the "witnesses chosen beforehand," the apostles and all those who by the Holy Spirit are to come to faith on the basis of the apostolic testimony. In faith they all are to see Christ's glory, which is hidden to the world until that day when it will be revealed to all people when He comes to judge the living and the dead.

6.

"This sacrament *is* the Gospel." Luther's recognition matches perfectly what the New Testament teaches. "For as often as you eat this bread and drink the cup, you proclaim (*kataggellete* is to be taken as present, not as imperative) the Lord's death until He comes." Thus Paul writes at the end of the first and oldest account we have of the institution of the Lord's Supper. Several of the ancient liturgies quote these words of 1 Cor. 11:26 as if they were a part of the account itself that Paul is quoting here [*Ap. Con.* 8. 12]. For the passage at 1 Cor. 11:23ff. belongs to the "traditions" that the apostle "received" and had faithfully passed on, just as the passage at 15:3ff., which reminds us of the Second Article of the Creed. That Paul received his Gospel directly from the Lord and not from men (Gal. 1:12) does not at all preclude his coming to know of details in the life of Jesus and the texts used in the liturgy by way of the church, probably in Antioch. The words "I received [*parelabon*] from the Lord what I also delivered [*paredōka*] to you" contain the same technical terms that we find in 1 Cor. 15:3 and probably mean no more than that what Paul hands on goes back to Jesus' Last Supper and what He Himself said and did there. Evidence of the utter reliability and great age of this account may be seen in the fact that it records an item that is no longer found in Mark. It was no longer regarded as essential that at the institution Jesus distributed the bread during the meal while the cup came at the end. Whether verse 26 belongs to the ancient account itself or is an authoritative commentary of the apostle, it does say with incisive brevity that the Lord's Supper is the Gospel itself.

Baptism is the Gospel, because the whole Gospel is contained in it, not only in words but also in what our Redeemer does in His mighty rescue of us from sin, death and the devil. Absolution is the Gospel, the forgiveness of sins, the anticipation of the verdict of justification that will come in the last judgment. The Lord's Supper is also the Gospel, and indeed in quite a special way. The Gospel is the Good News proclaimed in all the world in these last days (Matt. 24:14; Acts 2:17; Heb. 1:2). It is the message of the incarnation of the eternal Word, of His redeeming death, His resurrection and ascension, His sitting at the right hand of the Father and His return in glory for the final judgment and to complete our redemption in our own resurrection.

It is the will of Christ that this Gospel be proclaimed to all peoples. But this proclamation is not only to be the message of what God has done in the past and what He will do in the future. The proclamation of this "eternal Gospel" (Rev. 14:6) is always to be accompanied by the celebration of the Sacrament that our Lord instituted, by which His death is proclaimed until He comes. Without the celebration of this Sacrament the proclamation of the Gospel could be understood as just one of the many religious messages in the world. This does indeed happen where people are ignorant of the Sacrament. Without the continual proclamation of the Gospel this Sacrament may be understood as just one of the many fellowship rites that exist in the world of religions or as an unintelligible action of a mystery religion. But the Gospel is more than a religious message, the Sacrament of the Altar more than a religious ceremony. Both the Gospel that is preached and the Gospel that occurs in the Sacrament contain one and the same gift, though in different forms: the forgiveness of sins. This is not some doctrine about the possibility of a forgiveness of sins, not an illustration of such a possibility, but the actual forgiveness itself, this unfathomable miracle of God's mercy that blots out our guilt and gives us everything that comes with forgiveness: life and salvation, redemption of the whole person, both soul and body. Both the Gospel and the Sacrament bring this forgiveness, for in both the Lamb of God who died for the sin of the world is present.

7.

And so we come to the question of the *Real Presence*, which we must touch on here at least briefly. Why was this for Luther the question about the Gospel itself? The Lord Christ is present in all the means of grace. He comes to us in the preaching of the Gospel, in Baptism, and in absolution. In these He is present in His church, which is His body. Also where two or three are gathered in His name, gathered around His Word and Sacrament, there is the body of Christ, the whole body. For the body of Christ is not some sort of organism. It cannot be separated into pieces. It is always completely present, just as the sacramental body is always completely present in each part of the consecrated bread.

> Whether one this bread receiveth
> Or a thousand, still He giveth
> One sure food that does not fail.

Luther and our Lutheran fathers loved to quote these words from Aquinas's "Lauda Sion salvatorem." They ring on in the Communion hymns of our church. They can and must be applied in an analogous way to the "mystical body," the church, in order to avoid the unbiblical, romantic theory of the church as an organism. The presence in the Sacrament of the Altar, however, is not the same as the presence in the other means of grace.

There is today a most earnest struggle going on to understand this presence. There are Catholic and Protestant theologians who speak of it as making Christ's death, Christ's passion contemporary, a re-presentation of His sacrificial death. Among Catholic theologians such theories emerge from the effort to clarify the doctrine of Trent that identifies the sacrifice on the cross with the sacrifice in the Mass. According to the doctrine of Trent the sacrifice of Mass is to be understood as *memoria*, *repraesentatio*, and *applicatio* of the sacrifice on Golgotha. It was the late Benedictine monk, Odo Casel, who propounded the mystery theory that has engaged so much discussion. The point of departure for his exposition of the "cultic mystery" was the Hellenistic mysteries. These are then seen as "shadows" of the future mysteries of the church, corresponding to the relationship between nature and supernature [*Übernatur*].

> The *Kyrios* of a mystery is a God who has entered into human misery and struggle, has made his appearance on earth (epiphany) and fought here, suffered, even been defeated; the whole sorrow of mankind in pain is brought together in a mourning for the God who must die. But then in some way comes a return to life through which the God's companions, indeed the whole of nature revives and lives on. This was the way of pious faith and the sacred teaching (*hieros logos*), of society in the earliest mystical age. But the world, society is always in need of life; so the epiphany goes on and on in worship; the saving, healing act of God is performed over and over. Worship [*Kult*] is the means of making it real once more, and thus of breaking through to the spring of salvation. The members of the cult present again in a ritual, symbolic fashion, that primeval act. . . .

The mystery, therefore, embraces in the first place the broad concept of ritual *"memorial"—anamnēsis, commemoratio*—the ritual performance and *making present [Gegenwärtigsetzung]* of some act of the God's, upon which rests the existence and life of a community. (*Das Christliche Kultmysterium*, 2d ed. [1935]; emphasis added [*The Mystery of Christian Worship* (1962), 53]).

Justin and the early church could never have dreamed up something like this, certainly not if they remained in agreement with Paul, who did not regard these mysteries as earlier stages of Christian worship but as demonic perversion of divine truth. This whole theory falls to pieces before the simple fact that while the Hellenistic mysteries rest on myths, the Sacrament of the Altar is a matter of history. When did Attis and Osiris live? When did they die? The question is senseless because the myth does not tell of historical events. Jesus Christ, however, is a historical person. His death is a historical event that happened outside the gates of Jerusalem "under Pontius Pilate." The women who went to find His body did not have to wander all around like Cybele and Isis in the myth. They knew the place of His grave. And His resurrection was also a historical event: "On the third day He rose again from the dead." The whole theory was constructed to provide a foundation for the dogma of the identity of the sacrifice on the cross and the sacrifice of the Mass as defined by Trent. But where is there any such foundation in the New Testament? Is it by chance that the passage in the New Testament putting the high priestly work of Christ at the center has the word "once" [*ephapax*] right at the crucial place? He "entered *once* for all into the Holy Place, taking not the blood of goats and calves but His own blood, thus securing an eternal redemption" (Heb. 9:12). Who dares to interpret away this "once" in view of the words that conclude this great chapter: "Just as it is appointed for men to die *once*, and after that comes judgment, so Christ, having been offered *once* to bear the sins of many, will appear a second time, not to deal with sin but to save those who are eagerly waiting for Him" (Heb. 9:27f.).

Casel's theory is therefore untenable. It can be accommodated in the Roman Church because, for one thing, it has a different relationship with heathen religion than we do, and for another, because its doctrine of the real presence is not in any way challenged by it. That is not the case with similar theories that have sprung up in Protestant soil and today even make an impression on Lutherans. Casel betrays a very significant uncertainty regarding the Biblical concept of remembrance, as is shown by his opinion of Passover.

> God's prescriptions were carried in exact ritual: the paschal lamb eaten
> in travelling clothes; *the history read recalling* how they left the land
> where they were slaves. So Israel's salvation and the founding of God's
> people was celebrated each year in ritual. . . . But the passover use
> was not properly a mystery because it was related first of all to human
> events and a *human deliverance.* (Casel, 60 [*Mystery*, 31])

What a misunderstanding this is of *salvation history* [*Heilsgeschichte*]
and *salvation facts* [*Heilstatsachen*] in the Biblical sense!

In his thoughtful study, "The Salvation Event in the Proclamation
of the Word and in Holy Communion" (in *Grundlegung des Abend-
mahlsgesprächs* [1954], 35–79 [for the English see his *Worship in the
Name of Jesus* (St. Louis, 1968), 141–96]), Peter Brunner points out
the realization of the presence of salvation history in the cultus that was
first propounded by Rudolf Otto and developed by Old Testament scholars like Mowinckel, von Rad, and Weiser. It is expressed in the words
of Moses in Deut. 5:1f.:

> Hear, O Israel, the statutes and the ordinances which I speak in your
> hearing *this day*, and you shall learn them and be careful to do them.
> The Lord our God *made a covenant with us* in Horeb. *Not with our
> fathers* did the Lord make this covenant, but *with us*, who are all of
> us *here* alive *this day*. The Lord spoke with you face to face at the
> mountain, out of the midst of the fire, while *I stood between the Lord
> and you at that time, to declare to you the Word of the Lord.*

The interpretation that von Rad gives of this "actualization of the redemptive events" in the cultus and in God's holy Word that is part of
the cultus is found in P. Brunner, p. 38 [*Worship*, 145]. It is really true
that those who eat the Passover, in which they remember a historical
event, are present at this event, because it is "salvation history," the
history of what God had done, for which there is no temporal time. In
addition to the way in which a past event is made a present reality
through the Word, the Old Testament also has parabolic actions by the
prophets, such as in Ezekiel 4 and 5, something still seen in the New
Testament in the action of Agabus in Acts 21:10f. This *oth* [Hebrew],
a holy sign (the word is also used of God's miraculous deeds), for the
people of the Old Testament is really more than just a parable. R. Otto
has called it "an effective representation" [*The Kingdom of God and the
Son of Man* (Boston, 1957), 302]. He and others have used this then as
the way to explain the Lord's Supper. The sacrifice of Christ's death,
anticipated at the Last Supper, is re-presented in the celebration of the

Sacrament, just as also from the opposite perspective the messianic banquet in heaven is anticipated in it. This has been used by Anglican theologians, and even by some Lutherans, to take the hazardous step of seeing in the Sacrament the "re-presentation" of Christ's sacrifice and in this way seeing the Sacrament itself as a sacrifice. There was indeed a reality inherent in a prophetic sign, as also in the prophetic Word. It makes no difference whether the fall of Jerusalem is proclaimed by Jeremiah by "word" or by "action." But the category of parabolic action or of *oth* simply cannot explain the Lord's Supper. This is indicated by the fact that those theologians who explain it in this way no longer have any appreciation for the actual presence of the body and blood of Christ. Their doctrine of the Real Presence is Calvinistic, and that of the sacrifice is Roman Catholic. When it happens that they become Roman Catholic, they then have no difficulty in accepting transubstantiation.

There must be something else that is unique about the real presence in the Lord's Supper. The death of Christ is indeed a unique historical event. As with every actual event in earthly history, it is unrepeatable. But at the same time, like the exodus from Egypt commemorated in the Passover, it is also God's redemptive act, something that stands outside of earthly time, which does not exist for God. Rev. 13:8 calls Christ "the Lamb slain from the foundation of the world" [KJV]. He is the Crucified not simply as *staurōtheis* (aorist, which signifies a single event) but as the *estaurōmenos* (perfect, which means that what happened continues in effect). We note how Paul uses the aorist and perfect, comparing, for example, 1 Cor. 1:13 with 1:23; 2:2, 8; 2 Cor. 13:4 with Gal. 3:1; etc. From this we may see that with God a "temporal" event can be "eternal." But as a general principle this may be said of all God's deeds. What applies to Golgotha applies also to Sinai according to Deut. 5:2. However illuminating may be the recognition that in the Bible God's deeds in the past have also a present reality, this does not explain what is the *proprium* of the Sacrament. Brunner acknowledges this when he says that re-presentation and the Real Presence go together. "Through the real presence of Jesus' body and blood the *repraesentatio* carried out in Holy Communion receives its real and present concretion" (*Grundlegung*, 64 [*Worship*, 177]). The question that Brunner leaves open is what the actual "body" and "blood" are that are received under the forms of bread and wine. This is where I must part company with him, even though he quotes my statement in *Vom Sakrament des Altars* (p. 69) in support of his view (*Grundlegung*, 64 [*Worship*, 178]). The context of my statement shows that we are not in agreement.

Brunner says (p. 63 [*Worship*, 177]) "that the *sacrificed* body and the atoning and covenant-effecting *sacrificial* blood and, with this, Jesus' sacrifice on the cross, are present to us under the Eucharistic food and presented [*dargereicht*] with the bread and the wine" (Brunner's emphasis). Why is sacrifice stressed so much? There is no doubt that we receive the *sacrificed* body and the *sacrificed* blood. But why is it not said that the sacrificed body is at the same time the glorified body? It is certainly true that, along with the Christ who was sacrificed for us, His sacrifice on the cross is present—along with the one who suffered [*Christus passus*] comes also His suffering [*passio Christi*]. But can the sacrifice of the cross be *distributed* [*dargereicht*, that is, to the communicants]? If I have misunderstood Brunner, I would ask him in sincere friendship to clear up the misunderstanding. And I would put to him the question, What do unbelievers receive, that is, with the mouth? And how can something be possible today that the church regarded as impossible for 1,700 years and that is still today regarded by most of Christendom as impossible, namely, that there can be fellowship at the Lord's Supper between those who confess that the consecrated bread *is* the body of the Lord and those who confess no more than that the bread is a *sign* of the body, as is the case with those who hold to the Heidelberg Catechism. In his careful and conscientious investigation of the question (*Grundlegung*, 11–33) Brunner concedes that his approval of altar fellowship between Lutherans and those who confess the Heidelberg Catechism would not have been shared by Luther, had he known of this catechism (*Grundlegung*, 32 n. 25). But does this disagreement between Brunner and Luther perhaps relate to a deeper disagreement in understanding the essence of the Real Presence?

8.

Here we must break off the discussion of the Real Presence. Our intention was to substantiate Luther's statement: "This sacrament is the Gospel." If this is so, then it is clear that the church cannot exist without it. It had such vital place in the divine service in the time of the apostles, in the ancient church, in the Middle Ages, and also in Lutheranism before the incursion of Pietism. The divine service was the "Mass," a service of the Word and at the same time a service of the Sacrament. There is a growing conviction in all Protestant churches that with the conscious dissolution of the Mass among the Reformed churches and its decline in Lutheranism, something has been lost that is essential to the church. There is something of the truth to the saying often heard in America: "If a Protestant goes to church, he finds a preacher; if a Catholic goes to church, he finds Christ." Preaching can only decline, can only lose its essence as the proclamation of the *Gospel*, if the Sacrament of the Altar no longer gives us the objective presence of the incarnate Christ, if we no longer receive His true body and His true blood. On the other hand in the Roman Church the decline in the proclamation of the Gospel has changed the character of the Sacrament. It is something marvelous to behold in a Cistercian abbey when the monks, after choral prayer together early in the morning, go into the sacristy, take off their cowls, put on their chasubles, and each goes by himself to his altar in the great church to celebrate his Mass, to offer the Holy Sacrifice, as they say. But is this impressive celebration still the Mass of the early church, not to mention the Sacrament of the New Testament? No one has more effectively criticized this development of the Mass, in which the praying church [*ecclesia orans*] disappears, than the leaders of the liturgical movement in the Catholic Church. I know an Anglican monastery, which is also a theological seminary, where the students go to Communion every morning but for months on end hear no sermon. Can the Gospel survive in such churches? The early church was a preaching church, as was also the church of the Middle Ages at the high points of its history. Certainly the juxtaposition of preaching—in the early church there were often several sermons—and the Eucharist has always presented a practical problem, even in the East where there seems to be plenty of time. The pressure of time led either to the sermon's being cut short, as in today's Catholic High Mass on Sunday, or to the establishment of special preaching services without the Sacrament on Sunday afternoon as in the late Middle Ages or as is still the case today with Vespers. It is by no means the case that only we Lutherans are plagued with the problem of finding the rightful place for both preaching and the Sacrament of the Altar in the Sunday divine service.

Another question is closely related to this one, namely, the congregation's communion. In the ancient church all who took part in the Mass of the Faithful received communion. This later came to an end when masses of people came streaming into the church, and Communion was often replaced by the distribution of bread that was blessed but not consecrated at the end of the service. In the Middle Ages Communion was very infrequent. To receive Communion four times a year—at the three high festivals and at one lesser one—was a sign of the highest piety. Even of monks was no more required. I once greatly astonished a Dominican when I explained that Thomas certainly did not celebrate Mass every day. Receiving Communion was replaced by adoration of the host, a practice unknown in the ancient church and still not practiced by the Eastern Church.

Just as customs changed in the early church in connection with Baptism (the baptizing of infants and adults), so there was also a change in church customs with regard to the Lord's Supper. Over many centuries pastoral care has wrestled with the problem of whether frequent or less frequent but more devoutly prepared-for Communion is preferred. There were already debates about this in the Middle Ages. Later the Jansenists and the Jesuits were in controversy about it, until at the beginning of this century the decision came down in favor of frequent, and where possible, daily communion. But this was at the cost of not taking sin seriously, since according to Catholic doctrine no one may receive the Sacrament who is in a state of mortal sin. This same problem arises in the Lutheran Church when frequent communion, going to the Lord's Supper at each divine service is urged, or when the participants in church gatherings are more or less morally compelled to go to the Table of the Lord without a serious confession preceding it, as our Confessions encourage it. For the *exploratio* of Augsburg Confession XXIV is expressly described in the Apology in such a way that it includes confession: "In our churches Mass is celebrated every Sunday and on other festivals, when the Sacrament is offered to those who wish for it after they have been examined and absolved" (Ap XXIV 1). This confession previously took place on Saturday and still does in many a congregation. To give this up or to let it rise or fall in the general confession of sins of the congregation would be a corruption of the Lutheran Sacrament and would open the door to a false understanding of the Lord's Supper. If appeal is made to the Catholic liturgy, then it must be remembered that there also confession is to precede Communion, although it does so differently because of the different understanding of sin.

If we ask ourselves what we as pastors can do about these questions, we should take comfort from the fact that we are not the first to have to struggle with the problem of "Word and Sacrament, Preaching and Holy Communion." The church has always faced the needs indicated by these questions. So we have to beware of liturgical experiments, both the serious and the silly. The latter do exist, as when Bishop Lilje's *Sonntagsblatt* recently published a letter that reported a new way to celebrate the Lord's Supper. When the congregation sat around a table for the Lord's Supper, they left one place empty for the coming Lord.

That is a Jewish custom practiced in all pious Jewish homes in the East. At the festive Sabbath meal or some other festival a place is always kept open for the coming Messiah. What ignorance about the meaning of the Lord's Supper and the liturgy is to be found in our congregations! The need is not met by the artificial liturgical constructions of some High Church people. The great learning of modern liturgics is of no help either unless its fruits are translated into the plain language of the people, as Pius Parsch of Klosterneuberg on the Catholic side has done in splendid fashion for German-speaking people.

Why do we not explain the liturgy to our congregations, especially to the youth? That naturally presumes that we know the teaching of our church regarding the divine service, that we ourselves study the old church orders with their liturgical treasures, that we understand the Lutheran way of combining loyalty to the old liturgical heritage with the great Gospel freedom of which Article 10 for the Formula of Concord speaks. We do not mean liturgical arbitrariness but authentic Gospel freedom. We have to face the fact that a heritage that has been lost over 250 years cannot be restored quickly. We must have several forms of the divine service, just as the Roman Church has and practices in the preservation of unfamiliar rites. We need small circles and congregations in which the old liturgical heritage is preserved along with confession—*confessio* always means confession of the faith, confession of sins, and praise of God all in one—as is done in such an exemplary way, a way that puts us all to shame, in the "Brethren" congregations in Braunschweig. Moreover, in the large congregations we need extensive instruction in the liturgy. We need preaching services and special services of Holy Communion. We particularly need the divine service in the sense of the Lutheran Mass with both preaching and the celebration of the Sacrament. The sermon will then need to be short, but above all it must be authentic proclamation of the Gospel. There can be no renewal of the Lord's Supper without renewed preaching, preaching that is not just the pious talk of a man but disciplined exposition of Holy Scripture that strikes the heart. Such preaching grows out of serious study of Scripture, plumbing the depths of the divine Word. It should not be that the hearer of the text will always know exactly what is coming next because he has already heard it a hundred times.

Such are the tasks set before us, and no one can relieve us of them, neither hierarchy nor synod nor theological faculty. From the inner renewal of our office, the *ministerium docendi evangelii et porrigendi sacramenta* (ministry of teaching the Gospel and administering the sacraments), the primary office of the church, the only one that the Lord Himself has instituted, can the renewal of our church come. *Veni creator Spiritus!*

HOLY BAPTISM

Letters to Lutheran Pastors, No. 4
March 1949

(Published in *In Statu Confessionis: Gesammelte Aufsätze von Hermann Sasse*, ed. Friedrich Wilhelm Hopf [Berlin and Hamburg: Lutherisches Verlagshaus, 1966], 91–100.)

With the doctrine of *Holy Baptism* the difference between the confessions that appeal to the Reformation has become clear to many of our contemporaries. Already in the 16th century, besides the controversy over the Lord's Supper, there was a very lively, revealing debate over Baptism, above all at the Mömpelgard Colloquy between Andreae and Beza. But since Lutherans and Reformed retained and defended the practice of infant baptism against the Baptists, it was not sufficiently noticed at that time what a profound difference existed between the confessions also in the understanding of this means of grace. We have to thank Karl Barth for putting his finger on what for him was "a wound on the body of the church" ("Die kirchliche Lehre von der Taufe," *Theol. Existenz heute*, New Series 4, 1947; *Theol. Studien*, part 14, 28f.). And even if he encounters determined opposition to his charge that the Reformed churches would like to revise their teaching and practice of Baptism, it remains an open question whether Barth has not been more Reformed on this subject than the Reformed, whether he has not seen more clearly than any Reformed theologian before him certain inconsistencies of Zwingli and Calvin, who expressed themselves in terms of their opposition to the Anabaptists of the 16th century. It is necessary for us Lutherans to deal with the understanding of Baptism and with Barth's objections to infant baptism because Barth's pupils have tried to read his doctrine of Baptism into the Augsburg Confession and because considerable uncertainty about the basis of infant baptism and therefore about the understanding of the sacrament itself can be seen in current Lutheran dogmatics.

1.

Basic to every discussion about the Sacrament of Baptism is the recognition that Baptism is a *sacrament*, a means of grace in the strict sense. It is not just a more or less beautiful, more or less legitimate custom of the church just like confirmation, marriage, and burial. Thus all arguments collapse immediately that see in Baptism a symbolic action, perhaps the symbol of the prevenient grace [*gratia praeveniens*] that precedes all human action or a symbol of what makes "a church comprising all the people" [*Volkskirchentum*] in contrast with what Troeltsch calls "sects," in the sense of a second form of Reformation church that emerged out of the radical Anabaptist movement. Nowadays people speak of "free churches" rather than "sects" and maintain that the abandonment of infant baptism would destroy the *Volkskirche* and lead to the "free church."

Now in fact all the "free churches" except the Baptists practice infant baptism. Quite apart from this, however, the very serious dogmatic question must be raised, whether the Sacrament of Baptism can be used as a means of maintaining the *Volkskirche* even though infant baptism may not be theologically defensible. Baptism has been a part of Christian dogmatics since the days of the apostles. The concept of a *Volkskirche* is scarcely a hundred years old. As far as we know, this theologically illegitimate term was coined by Johann Hinrich Wichern. At any rate he gave currency to the idea from the sociology of religion. The theological nonsense of this term, which no educated theologian should utter, is apparent when the assertion is made repeatedly that one becomes a member of a free church by voluntary decision, whereas one is "born into" the *Volkskirche*.

One never becomes a member of the church by a decision or by birth. The latter is taken to be the case only in certain state churches, such as that of Zurich. In this prototype of a *Volkskirche* from Zwingli's time, one may exercise all the rights of a member of the church, with the exception of what is reserved to the clergy, even without being baptized. According to the witness of the New Testament (1 Cor. 12:13) one becomes a member of the church by Baptism. The only theologically legitimate question, on which the rightness or wrongness of infant baptism depends, is who is to be baptized, people who are able to confess their faith in Jesus Christ, that is, adults and older children, or also minor children, that is, infants in the proper sense of the term.

2.

So the question of infant baptism is a theological question and not merely a practical, sociological question. It is also not a question that can simply be answered historically. Thomas Aquinas (*Summa th.* 3, question 68, 9) answers the objection that intention and faith are necessary for the reception of Baptism, and therefore that children cannot be baptized, with a quotation from the last chapter of *The Celestial Hierarchy* of Dionysius the Areopagite, according to whom the apostles approved of infant baptism. That is a tradition that, to say the least, is beyond verification. But Joachim Jeremias (*Hat die älteste Christenheit die Kindertaufe geübt?* [1938] [translated as *Infant Baptism in the First Four Centuries* (1960)]) and W. F. Flemington (*The New Testament Doctrine of Baptism* [1948]) with an abundance of persuasive arguments have made it seem likely that infant baptism, which is first explicitly spoken of by Irenaeus (about 185), goes back to the time of the apostles. There it would have been practiced according to the model of the Jewish baptism of proselytes. This we know was performed not only on adults, but in the case of the conversion of whole families it was performed on all who belonged to the whole "house" and so included the children. The well-known examples of Lydia, the dealer in purple, and of the jailer at Philippi (Acts 16), who were baptized with their whole household after they themselves had come to faith, would be relevant. When Polycarp testified at his martyr's trial that he had served the Lord for 86 years (*Mart. Pol.* 9), that can only refer to his membership in the church. Then his baptism would have occurred in the apostolic age, before the year 70. The assertion of Justin (*Apol.* 1. 15) that in his day there were many Christians in their sixties and seventies "who had become disciples of Christ as children" can only refer to people who were baptized as children between A.D. 80 and 90. Of Ireneaus we have spoken already. He confesses that Christ came to save all, "all who through Him are born again to God: infants, little children, boys, youths, and men" (*Adv. haer.* 2. 22. 4). In the church order of his pupil Hippolytus the baptism of little children is explicitly mentioned. They are to be baptized prior to the adults, and their parents or a relative are to represent them in giving consent and in the confession of the creed by speaking for them in their place (*Apost. trad.* 46). When Tertullian in his writing *On Bap-*

tism explicitly opposes the custom of infant baptism, he does not speak against it as if it were an innovation. So also later when Pelagius attacks Augustine's doctrine of original sin, he lets the point stand that children also are baptized and does not contest infant baptism. Similarly Origen and Cyprian take the baptism of children for granted. Origen stated that infant baptism goes back to a tradition the apostles received from the Lord (*Commentary on Romans* 5. 9), a statement that was transmitted to the Middle Ages by Dionysius the Areopagite. Cyprian gives Bishop Fidus the well-known advice that Baptism is not to be delayed until the eighth day after birth according to the analogy of circumcision (*Ep.* 64). Jeremias is right when he maintains that a later introduction of infant baptism would have provoked a profound upset in the church and would have left distinct traces in the history of the church. What we know of the history of the church indicates much rather that in the early church both forms of baptism, the baptism of adults and infant baptism, always existed side by side, just as they do today in the mission fields. This can only mean that infant baptism must go back to the time of the apostles. It would have been included in the practice of baptizing whole families to which the New Testament gives witness, even though children are not explicitly mentioned.

3.

If we must then answer yes with the greatest probability to the historical question, whether the church of the apostolic age knew and practiced infant baptism, we have still in no way decided the theological question, whether it is right to baptize infants. Did not the church in Corinth in Paul's day practice also vicarious baptism for those who had died? We could be dealing with a very ancient misuse. Infant baptism has a theological foundation only if it can be shown from Scripture that it is a legitimate form of baptism.

The argument that once the Anabaptists and nowadays Karl Barth have raised against infant baptism asserts that to the essence of the Sacrament of Baptism belong "the responsible willingness and readiness of the baptized person to receive the promise of grace directed towards him and to be party to the pledge of allegiance concerning the grateful service demanded of him" [Barth, *The Teaching of the Church Regarding Baptism* (1948), 40]. In an article in the Berlin church weekly *Die Kirche* a pupil of Barth recently tried to support this view by referring to the account of the Ethiopian chamberlain in Acts 8, where not only the expression of the desire of the one to be baptized but also his confession served as conditions for the baptism. That theologian had simply overlooked the fact that verse 37, with its request for a confession and the giving of a baptismal confession, is an old insertion, as examination of the manuscripts demonstrates. The oldest and best manuscripts are ignorant of it, and so they are witnesses of the fact that in earliest times (cf. Acts 2:41) a baptism was known in which a creed was not spoken.

Therefore, we have to ask, What is Baptism according to the witness of the New Testament? What does it give or what is the good of it? How is Baptism related to the faith of the one to be baptized? Is it necessary for salvation or not? What we may answer first of all is that according to the clear teaching of the New Testament Baptism is the "washing of regeneration." The early church, which always simply identified Baptism with regeneration, and the church of all times, with the exception of the Reformed communities, have understood Titus 3:5 in this way—and rightly so. There Baptism is "the washing of regeneration and renewal in the Holy Spirit." In Baptism the Holy Spirit is bestowed; we are "baptized into one body" (1 Cor. 12:13). According to Rom. 6:3, the baptized are baptized into Christ's death. Those are all realities that happen not alongside of Baptism but in it. Water baptism in the New Testament, as long as it is baptism into Christ, in the name of Christ, is Spirit baptism; it is a being born anew and at the same time from above "of water *and* the Spirit" (John 3:5). The New Testament knows nothing of a being born again without Baptism or apart from Baptism. Baptism is therefore not a sign but a means of regeneration. To regard it only as a sign of a regeneration that also may take place without it or apart from it is unbiblical.

What is it that prompts the Reformed doctrine? We may observe something similar in the doctrine of the Lord's Supper. On the one hand the pure symbolism of Zwingli is rejected. He saw Baptism as merely a sign professing that one is a Christian, just as the white cross worn on the garment of a Swiss Confederate made him recognizable as a Swiss Confederate [Library of Christian Classics, 24:131]. On the other hand, along with the Roman sacramental doctrine of an *opus operatum*, the Lutheran—and New Testament—identification of sign and action is also rejected.

At the bottom of all this lies the antipathy of Calvin and his predecessors in medieval theology against the idea that an external, physical action can produce spiritual effects, such as the forgiveness of sins. This is first of all a secular, philosophical presupposition, and second, it misunderstands the significance of the Word of God in Baptism. "For without the Word of God the water is simple water and no Baptism. But with the Word of God it is Baptism, that is, a gracious water of life and a washing of regeneration" (SC IV). Also in Catholic doctrine the Word as the *forma* is inseparably tied up with the sacrament; indeed, it is what makes the sacrament a sacrament. This is in harmony with the words of Augustine, which time and again are quoted by all churches in the West: "The word comes to the element and makes the sacrament." Where Luther differs from the Catholic doctrine of Baptism he says himself in the Smalcald Articles, distinguishing himself from both the Thomists and the Scotists:

> We do not agree with Thomas and the Dominicans who forget the Word [God's institution] and say that God has joined to the water a spiritual power which, through the water, washes away sin. Nor do we agree with Scotus and the Franciscans who teach that Baptism washes sin away through the assistance of the divine will, as if the washing takes place only through God's will and not at all through the Word and the water. (SA III V 2–3)

With Luther everything depends on the intimate connection of Word and water: "God is surely a God of life. Because He is there in this water, it cannot but be the very water of life, which puts death and hell to flight and makes alive with the life that has no end" (WA 52, 102, 29). Luther has no need to demonstrate first that this presence of God or Christ can be no other presence than that which happens in His Word. All effects of Baptism are effects of the Word combined with the water for Luther and for the Lutheran Church.

The Reformed opposition to this Lutheran understanding of Baptism is therefore nothing else than opposition to the Lutheran doctrine of the means of grace as a whole. They are opposing the fact that God does not give His Spirit, and therewith forgiveness of sins, life and salvation, to anyone apart from the external means of His grace, apart from the external Word, apart from Baptism, or apart from the Lord's Supper. "The power of Jesus Christ, which is the only power of Baptism, is *not bound* to the administration of Baptism" (Barth, 14f.). The earlier Reformed theologians favored the distinction between the external baptism with water and the inner baptism with the Holy Spirit and with the blood of Jesus Christ, which cleanses from all sin. But the two are not always received together; it is possible to have the one without the other. Whether a person receives the baptism of the Spirit and blood together with water baptism depends on whether he belongs to those who are predestined or not. Hence we can understand the consistent opposition ever since Calvin to emergency baptism and in particular baptism by midwives [Niesel, *Reformed Symbolics* (1962), 270]. In the Union Constitution of the Palatinate we find the sentence: "The Protestant Evangelical Christian Church of the Palatinate accepts no emergency baptism" (E. F. K. Müller, *Die Bekenntnisschriften der ev.-reformierten Kirche* [1903], 871). Baptism then gives the person nothing that he could not also have without Baptism. Whether one is saved or not does not at all depend on Baptism, but only on whether one is predestined to salvation or not. That is the classic Reformed doctrine. Even when the old doctrine of predestination is weakened or abandoned, as by the followers of Barth, its consequence still remains: Baptism is indeed instituted by Christ—Calvin accepts the institution of Baptism by Christ in agreement with Luther and with the whole ecclesiastical tradition of the Eastern and Western church—and it must be done in the church as an ordinance of Christ, but Baptism is not necessary for salvation. One can, Barth maintains (p. 15), speak only of a necessity of command [*necessitas praecepti*], not a necessity of means [*necessitas medii*].

4.

When the Lutheran Church against this position affirms the *necessitas medii*, the character of Baptism as a means of grace in the strict sense, it is naturally not in conflict with the old Catholic statement: "God is not confined to His sacraments." That God may have other ways of saving people has never been questioned by our church, as the writings of Luther and the classical Lutherans on the fate of children who died unbaptized proves. But He has not revealed anything to us about that, and we are bound to what He has revealed to us. What we must be on our guard against is the tearing apart of Spirit and Word, of external and internal baptism. It is water baptism inseparably bound to God's Word of which Luther's baptismal hymn speaks:

All that the mortal eye beholds
Is water as we pour it.
Before the eye of faith unfolds
The power of Jesus' merit.
For here it sees the crimson flood
To all our ills bring healing;
The wonders of his precious blood

The love of God revealing,
Assuring his own pardon.

How the marvel of the rebirth that is worked through Baptism relates to the fact that baptized people also are lost is hidden in divine predestination, about which the Gospel has revealed nothing to us. We shall understand that much better in the light of glory, as Luther says at the end of his *Bondage of the Will*. We cling to the Gospel and to the promises that the Gospel attaches to Baptism when we confess of Baptism as the washing of regeneration: "It works forgiveness of sins, delivers from death and the devil, and gives eternal salvation to all who believe this, as the words and promises of God declare" (SC IV).

But what of the faith of the child to be baptized? With this question we come to the heart of the Reformed rejection of the Lutheran doctrine of Baptism. This rejection has its parallels in the Reformed world in the so-called Gorham controversy regarding Baptism a century ago when the denial of baptismal regeneration by the Evangelicals in the Church of England deeply troubled Anglicanism. If one stands for infant baptism, then the following alternative seems to be inescapable: Either Baptism bestows forgiveness of sins and regeneration to eternal life apart from the personal faith of the child being baptized and his personal confession—that is the answer of the Catholic Church, which lets the faith of the church take the place of the faith of the child to be baptized— or forgiveness of sins and regeneration are detached from the administration of Baptism. In practical terms this opens several possibilities of viewing Baptism. One can with the majority of the Reformed retain infant baptism, thereby seeing in it the New Testament sign of the covenant analogous to Old Testament circumcision, referring to Col. 2:11. Or one can reject infant baptism altogether as was done by the Anabaptists at the time of the Reformation and is done today by the "congregations of Christians baptized as believers" [*Gemeinden gläubig getaufter Christen*]. Or one can take a middle way with Karl Barth between these possibilities. He declares infant baptism as valid but as a violation of the New Testament order of Baptism, a false ordering of baptismal practice that rests on the erroneous presuppositions of a *Volkskirche* and must be revised by ecclesiastical decision. We need not here pursue the fact that Barth himself came to recognize that none of the large Reformed churches is disposed to follow his advice and give up the custom of baptizing infants that has been firmly established since Zwingli and Calvin. We might just ask in passing whether the position of the Baptists is not the real consequence of the Reformed doctrine of Baptism and whether the retention of infant baptism was not a compromise resulting from the power of a tradition that was a millennium and a half old and from their opposition to the Enthusiasts of the 16th century. For Baptism cannot be understood as the counterpart to circumcision, despite Col. 2:11, because circumcision lacks the very thing that makes Baptism Baptism. At the very least they are as different as the new covenant is from the old, as Israel according to the flesh is from Israel according to the Spirit. If one sticks to these parallels, then Baptism can never be more than a sign of grace. It can never be a means of grace in the fullest sense, even though the Reformed have tried to retain this term for Baptism.

As was often the case, Luther's way was the lonely way between Rome and the Enthusiasts. Over against the Enthusiasts, among whom he lumped Zwingli and his followers, as he would also have done with the Calvinists had they been part of his experience, he firmly held to the Sacrament of Baptism and everything that belongs with it: infant baptism, necessity for salvation, and regeneration. Over against Rome he firmly held to the *sola fide:* Forgiveness of sins, life, and salvation are given only to faith. Just as in the Sacrament of the Altar only *he* receives forgiveness of sins and so also life and salvation who has faith in "these words," that is, in the promise: "Given and shed for you for the forgiveness of sins," so it is true of Baptism: "It works forgiveness of sins, delivers from death and the devil and gives eternal salvation to all who *believe* this, as the words and promises of God declare." And this is not talking about some future faith that is then confessed at confirmation, so that this would be a necessary completion of Baptism.

Bucer, who first introduced pietistic ideas into the church, brought an un-Lutheran element into confirmation, which has its own rightful place, an idea rooted not in Biblical thought but in a sociological view of the church. This element ripened in the age of Pietism and rationalism. It is significant that in Wittenberg in the 18th century confirmation was introduced into the synagogue, not the church, where they were content with first communion. At that time people could only conceive of the church as an "association," a "religious society" that one joined by a voluntary decision.

Against all this for Luther the faith that is spoken of in connection with infant baptism is not the future faith of children to be reared as Christians nor is it, as many a Lutheran in the 19th century thought, a faith that is like a seed awakened to life by the act of baptism, but it is the faith with which the children come to baptism, just as with adults, except that this faith of children is not yet a conscious faith that they can confess themselves.

In the Large Catechism Luther calls our attention to the fact that the faith of an adult also can never be the foundation of Baptism:

> I myself, and all who are baptized, must say before God: "I come here in my faith, and in the faith of others, nevertheless I cannot build on the fact that I believe and that many people are praying for me. On this I build, that it is Thy Word and command." Just so, I go to the Sacrament of the Altar not on the strength of my own faith, but on the strength of Christ's Word. . . . We do the same in infant Baptism. We bring the child with the purpose and hope that he may believe, and we pray God to grant him faith. But we do not baptize him on that account, but solely on the command of God. (LC IV 56–57)

And Luther bases this on the fact that all people can lie and deceive themselves, but not God, who has given the command to baptize. That God through His Holy Spirit can also give faith to a child, just as to an adult, cannot be questioned when we remember how Jesus blessed the children and presented a child to His disciples as an example. Yes, strictly speaking, even the faith of the greatest hero of faith, even the faith of an Athanasius or a Luther, is no greater than the faith of an infant.

Or when does the faith begin, on the basis of which we dare to baptize? Is it at the age when we nowadays have confirmation or when small children are able to make some confession of faith, as Thomas Müntzer wanted? We would be making a psychologically perceived fact out of the wondrous working of the Holy Spirit if we here set a temporal boundary on the sway of the Holy Spirit.

Here too Luther goes his lonely way between the hierarchical safeguards of Rome and the psychological safeguards of the Enthusiasts. It is the lonely way of the Reformer, who heeds only the Word of God and counts on this Word for everything, even for what is humanly impossible. Only in this way can he and the Lutheran Church hold together the objectivity of the sacrament and the *sola fide*, whereby we do not forget that justifying faith is not the matter of a single moment, but the substance of our whole lives. Such faith is not some act of our commitment to God that is particularly perceived and experienced in some isolated moments of our life. Rather, it is the constant though always clouded reliance on the Gospel's promise of grace. Repentance also, according to the Gospel, is not just a single act but goes on our whole life long. So also our Baptism is not an isolated act, but something that goes on in all our life. Being a Christian does not just mean that we were once baptized but that we live in the strength of our Baptism and again and again return to it. To the question, "What does such baptizing with water signify?" the Small Catechism gives the familiar answer: "It signifies that the Old Adam in us should, by daily contrition and repentance, be drowned and die with all sins and evil lusts and, again, a new man daily come forth and arise, who shall live before God in righteousness and purity forever" (SC IV). As we who are both sinners and righteous live by daily contrition and repentance, by the daily forgiveness of sin, so also the death and resurrection of Christ, that real though also incomprehensible anticipation of an eschatological experience that takes place in Baptism, is something that is intended for our whole life.

This is how Luther understood Baptism and the faith of those who are baptized over against Rome and the Enthusiasts. We do not simply grasp them in a moment, either in the moment when the Sacrament of Baptism is received or in the moment of confirmation or in any other moment of our lives that we might like to designate, but we grasp them, or should grasp them, throughout our whole lives, every day anew. Therefore Luther also knows no second sacrament that would have to complete Baptism, neither confirmation nor a repentance that would be anything else than a return to Baptism.

5.

The question of whether adults or infants are to be baptized, then, has become theologically unimportant, although it remains important for church practice. We can see now why this question plays no role in the New Testament or with Luther. Apart from the fact that adults to be baptized speak their consent and creed themselves, Baptism has always been done in the church "as if" those to be baptized desire it themselves and believe what is confessed in the baptismal creed. This "as if" belongs to the very essence of the matter and may not be explained away as liturgical traditionalism or ecclesiastical conservatism. We baptize children as if they were adults, just as we baptize adults as if they were children. Whatever the difference between adults and children may mean for us humans and our judgment of a person, it means nothing for God. Before Him a person is a person, either a child of Adam or a child of God, regardless of age. That is the more profound reason why all baptismal liturgies deal with the child "as if" he were an adult.

Only the Nestorian and the Reformed churches have produced specific liturgies for the baptism of children.

It was also baptismal practice until Calvin and the Reformed Church that it did not take place before the assembled congregation. In the early church the baptismal candidates received the Sacrament of Baptism outside the worship room, while the congregation was assembled to intercede for those to be baptized. That apparently did not happen just for the sake of propriety, for the Baptists administer the baptismal washing in the sight of the congregation. The place of the baptistry, whether it is an expanded baptismal well or a simple font, was always in front of the entrance to the church in former times. It is most interesting that Calvin himself, who, we believe, destroyed the dogmatic content of Baptism, brought Baptism out of the realm of the private and individual, out of the vestibule, as it were, into the sanctuary of the assembled congregation. He probably took that over, as so much else, from Bucer in Strasbourg, to whom the corresponding instruction in the Hessian church order of 1539 may be traced. That instruction is found again in later Reformed church orders, such as those of the Palatinate of 1563 and Bentheim of 1588. And so while the Reformed Church reserves the administration of baptism to the ministerial office and forbids emergency baptism by the laity, especially by women, right in the New Testament we see the performance of baptism as part of the apostolic office receding into the background. So the worship service combined with a baptism is passed off as a "sacramental worship service" in the Reformed Church and in the Protestantism of today that is considerably influenced by modern Calvinism. They forget that sacrament in the sense of a sacramental worship service purely and simply means the Lord's Supper, the Sacrament of sacraments. Luther's terminology gives abundant evidence of this. Naturally, the Christian congregation is free to perform baptism in the worship service. But Luther never designated a worship service in which a child was baptized in conjunction with the Creed as a sacramental worship service. A sacramental service for him was the Mass, the combination of service of the Word and Lord's Supper. In that he was at one with the whole church before him. Whatever reforms might be necessary to restore respect for the Sacrament of Baptism in the Lutheran Church of today, under no circumstances should our church let itself be diverted from the goal of restoring the proper sacramental service of the church of all times, also of the Lutheran Reformation. A deeper understanding and a new appreciation of Baptism is only possible through a return to what Luther's catechism,

47

on the basis of the New Testament, in simple faith teaches about Baptism as the washing of regeneration.

"Yet I do as a child who is being taught the Catechism," writes Luther in the Preface to the Large Catechism. "Every morning, and whenever else I have time, I read and recite word for word the Lord's Prayer, the Ten Commandments, the Creed, the Psalms, etc. I must still read and study the Catechism daily, yet I cannot master it as I wish, but must remain a child and pupil of the Catechism, and I do it gladly" (LC Pref 7–8). How well it would be with us Lutheran pastors, how well it would be with our church, if we paid more attention to this word and let it become active in our life and in our office! How many false conceptions of Lutheranism would be gone from our own souls, how many prejudices about our church on the part of the world would then vanish all by themselves! Kyrie eleison!

THE LORD'S SUPPER IN THE NEW TESTAMENT

1941

(Published in *Vom Sakrament des Altars: Lutherische Beiträge zur Frage des heiligen Abendmahls*, ed. Hermann Sasse [Leipzig: Verlag von Dörffling and Franke, 1941], 26–78.)

The Sources

Paul and Mark

Historical investigation of the Lord's Supper in the New Testament begins on firm ground with the report of its institution in 1 Cor. 11:23–25. This report is the earliest literary source for our knowledge of the origin of the Lord's Supper. (It is also "the oldest document of Christianity that bears witness to Christ's words in direct speech, as Werner Elert points out in *Der christliche Glaube*, 5th ed. [1960], 361.) It was written in the mid-50s and so at least 10 years before the composition of Mark's gospel.

Prompted by the abuses that took place in Corinth, Paul reminds the congregation of what he had once "delivered" to them regarding the origin and meaning of the Lord's Supper. This is what he had taught them already when the congregation was founded in the year 50, and we may assume that not only the content but also the wording of the crucial text was already the same at that time. For the verses at 11:23–25, in contrast to those that precede and those that follow, have been no more freely formulated by Paul as he dictated than the similarly introduced verses about the content of the Gospel at 1 Cor. 15:3ff. (Joachim Jeremias has shown the pre-Pauline Aramaic origin of 1 Cor. 15:3b–5 in *Die Abendmahlsworte Jesu* [1935], 72f. [*The Eucharistic Words of Jesus* (1966), 101–03].) In both cases we are dealing rather with sharply defined statements of the Pauline kerygma, and the statements about the institution of the Lord's Supper seem to have served not only catechetical but also liturgical purposes. We may suppose that in all the congregations of Paul's mission territory these words were recited when the Lord's Supper was celebrated. ("One is certainly entitled to the assumption that the oldest forms of a liturgical account of the institution underlie the corresponding narratives of the New Testament"—F. Hamm, "Die liturgischen Einsetzungsberichte," *Liturgiegeschichtl. Quellen und Forschungen* 23 [1928]: 2; cf. also J. Brinktrine, *Die heilige Messe*, 2d ed. [1934]: 18f., and A. Arnold, *Der Ursprung des christlichen Abendmahls im Lichte der neueren liturgiegeschichtlichen Forschung* [1937], 77.) They read as follows according to the oldest attainable text without the expansions of later manuscripts:

> The Lord Jesus on the night in which He was betrayed took the bread, gave thanks and broke it and said: "This is My body for you; this do in remembrance of me." In the same way also the cup after the meal with the words: "This cup is the new covenant in My blood. This do, as often as you drink it, in remembrance of Me."

What is the origin of these words? Did Paul formulate them himself for his congregations or did he find them already as an established formulation in the church? What is the origin of their content? How did Paul, or whoever formulated these sentences before him, know what happened on Jesus' last night? How did they know of the Lord's words and their meaning? The apostle himself gives the answer in the words with which he introduces that account: "I received from the Lord what I also delivered to you."

There has recently been much lively discussion of this *egō gar parelabon apo tou kuriou ho kai paredōka humin*. Lietzmann has espoused the view that is also predominantly that of Catholic and Reformation-orthodox exegesis. (For Catholic exegesis see Wilhelm Koch, *Das Abendmahl im N. T.* [Bibl. Zeitfragen IV 10], 30f. Old Lutheran theology thought that Paul learned his theology and so also his doctrine of the Lord's Supper in the third heaven [2 Cor. 12:2f.], e.g., *Kurtz Bekentnis und Artickel vom hl. Abendmal* [1574], folio E 1; Joh. Gerhard, *Ausführliche Schrifftmessige Erklerung der beyden Artikel von der hei-*

ligen Tauffe und von dem heiligen Abendmahl [Jena, 1610], 237.) According to this view, "I received from the Lord" is to be understood in accordance with what Paul says of his Gospel in Gal. 1:11f. "I did not receive it from man [*oude . . . para anthrōpou elabon*], nor was I taught it, but it came through a revelation of Jesus Christ." A contrary view is represented by Rudolf Otto, Gerhard Kittel, and J. Jeremias, the last two on the basis of their knowledge of the rabbinical principle of tradition and its terminology. "From the Lord" is then to be understood as indicating that not the risen Lord but the historical Jesus is the starting point of the tradition. In this view Paul would then mean that the tradition concerning what happened at the Last Supper and the words that Jesus spoke there came to him by way of an unbroken chain of witnesses right back to the historical event itself. Lietzmann conceives of it in this way: Paul knew the narrative from the tradition of the church. "But the Lord has revealed to him the essential meaning of this story" (Hans Lietzmann, *Messe und Herrenmahl* [1926], 255 [*Mass and Lord's Supper* (1979), 208]). Lietzmann sees in Paul the creator of a new type of Lord's Supper, but he does not challenge the fact that the apostle knew and used a tradition about the Last Supper of Jesus. Even if Paul had had the conviction, on the basis of a special revelation, of possessing a better understanding of the Lord's Supper than the church before him and the apostles who participated in Jesus' Last Supper—a question that we will have to discuss later—it would no more exclude knowledge of a human tradition regarding this Last Supper than his statement regarding the Gospel in Gal. 1:12, "I did not receive it from man," excludes the apparently contradictory statement about the content of the Gospel in 1 Cor. 15:3, "I delivered to you as of first importance what I also received," that is, the formulated teaching of the earliest church.

Even if we had no other text by which to test the reliability of the tradition reproduced by Paul in 1 Cor. 11:23–25, the following considerations would support its essential accuracy. Any statement made around the year 50 about the events that happened on Jesus' last night, no more than 20 years earlier, was subject to the judgment of eyewitnesses, that is, the original apostles who were still living. Every reader and hearer of the Pauline account knew where he could make sure of the authenticity of the statement that was offered. If Paul had taught something else than the original apostles regarding the origin of the Sacrament that formed the heart of the original Christian cultus, his Judaizing opponents would hardly have missed the opportunity to prove clearly the unreliability of what he proclaimed. (This obviates Lietzmann's suggestion that the type of the Lord's Supper observed in the original [Jerusalem] congregation was introduced in Corinth by Jewish Christians and that Paul then thought it necessary in 1 Cor. 11 to lead the congregation back to his understanding of the Lord's Supper [*Messe und Abendmahl*, 254 (*Mass and Lord's Supper*, 207–08)].)

If Paul in those verses is only handing on a tradition that was there before he was, it gains weight the older it is. If, as we assume, it was formulated for liturgical use, then it must indeed be supposed that the characteristic of liturgical language and liturgical style has influenced the formulation. The liturgy speaks neither the language of a notarized official document nor that of a history textbook. But that in no way changes the fact that it preserves historical facts in its language with great faithfulness and at its center has accurately retained the very words of Jesus.

The reliability of the tradition preserved in 1 Cor. 11:23–25, which is only presumed on the basis of internal characteristics, is substantiated through the happy circumstance that the New Testament contains a second account of Jesus' Last Supper in Mark 14:22–25 that is quite independent of the Pauline account but is essentially in complete agreement with it. We give the Marcan account, emphasizing those words that it has in common with the Pauline:

> And as they were eating, *He took bread*, and blessed, and *broke it*, and gave it to them, *and said*, "Take; *this is My body.*" *And* he took *the cup*, gave thanks, gave it to them, and they all drank of it. And *He said*, "*This is My blood of the covenant*, poured out for many. Truly, I say to you, I shall not drink again of the fruit of the vine until that day when I drink it new in the kingdom of God."

A comparison of the two texts produces the following: (1) We are dealing with two different traditions. The Marcan text does not derive from the Pauline, nor vice versa. The differences are too great for that. It is impossible to see why Mark would leave out the mandate to repeat or why Paul would substitute a different reflection on the meaning of the celebration (1 Cor. 11:26) for the word of Jesus about the prospect of the messianic meal. (2) Both texts see in Jesus' Last Supper the institution of the Lord's Supper in the church; Paul says this explicitly, Mark simply takes it for granted. (3) Both texts agree on the essentials of the action and on the essentials of the explanatory words about the bread and the cup. (4) Both also differ just at the words of explanation in a way that shows the Marcan text to be an older form of the tradition. If we can here find the rule borne out that liturgical texts are prone to grow, to comment on themselves, and to improve their form, then we must award the greater age to the Marcan text of the explanatory words as shorter, less clear, and less shaped to liturgical use (contrary to J. Behm, who in G. Kittel, *Theol. Wörterbuch zum N. T.* 3:730, lines 27ff. [*Theological Dictionary of the New Testament* 3:731], gives Paul the preference because the word about the cup in him shows an "inconceivable autonomy"). The explanatory word about the bread in Mark is in the shortest conceivable form: "This is My body." The Pauline text adds: "for you. Do this in remembrance of Me." At this point we simply point this out without discussing the question of whether the expansion of the wording under consideration in Paul changes the meaning of the Eucharistic words of Jesus or simply makes them clearer. Also in the case of the word about the cup, the wording of Mark must be regarded as earlier. Both texts in fact say the same thing: The wine that is the content of the cup is the blood of the covenant, that is, the blood that was poured out to complete the covenant. Jeremias suggests, "The strangely complicated formulation of the word over the wine in Paul/ Luke ('this cup is the new covenant') was occasioned by the intention of warding off the misunderstanding that the Lord's Supper was a Thyestian meal where blood was drunk" (*Die Abendmahlsworte Jesu* [1935], 60; cf. 58 [*Eucharistic Words*, 170; cf. 168–69]). He has also shown that the Pauline formulation of the word about the bread is, insofar as it goes beyond the Marcan text, impossible in Aramaic [*Eucharistic Words*, 185–86].

In summary then we may conclude that Christianity in the forties knew several independent versions of a tradition and used them in the celebration of the Lord's Supper. According to it, Jesus at His Last Supper gave His disciples bread and wine with the words: "This is My body," "This is My covenant blood, shed for many." This makes the credibility of the reports extraordinarily strengthened. But has it been proved? We have no further sources for the period between Jesus' Last Supper and the oldest account that was later included in the Gospel of Mark. May we assume that this oldest report goes back to the testimonies of the eyewitnesses, that is, the circle of the Eleven? From the sources that we have it is simply impossible to prove this. It would, however, be methodologically impermissible to deny the authenticity of the report until exact and direct proof of its reliability is furnished. The skepticism with which even the research in our part of that tradition has been confronted does not even provide evidence of the historical sense of its representatives. In this skepticism the historian, who with

Ranke wants to know how it actually was, is no longer speaking but the prosecuting attorney, who accepts no word of the man suspected of false witness unless proof is provided by eyewitnesses or circumstantial evidence. We must be clear about the fact that it means the end of *historical* investigation of the New Testament if the rule of all historical research is no longer valid, that a report is to be regarded as reliable until there are compelling grounds—and not mere conjectures—to question its accuracy. In our case this means: The traditions at hand in 1 Cor. 11 and Mark 14 about Jesus' Last Supper have a claim to credibility where they agree until compelling grounds are produced that they are legendary and falsely report what actually happened in that Last Supper of Jesus. Whether there are such grounds is a question the conscientious historian must take quite seriously. He may not shirk the responsibility of pursuing every trace of any such grounds. When he has done this and when his investigation of the New Testament comes up with no such grounds, then he has only the one possibility: that the reliability of that tradition is established indirectly.

Matthew and Luke

A sufficient ground for doubting the accuracy of the Marcan and Pauline tradition of Jesus' Last Supper and the origin of the Lord's Supper in the church that is based on it could exist if it could be shown that there is a divergent tradition in the New Testament, one that is otherwise construed at least in hints. Even then we would still have to explore carefully whether the early church did not have good grounds for placing more trust in the tradition represented by Mark and Paul than in this other one. But then the unique position of the account standing behind Mark and Paul would be shaken anyway. In fact there are those who think they have found a completely different tradition, and this in the account of the Lord's Supper in Luke.

While the account in Matthew (26:26–29) is a simple expansion of Mark 14:22–25, in which the most important variation is the addition of "for the forgiveness of sins" to the word about the cup, the text of Luke presents us with a puzzle that has not been solved to this day. It reads as follows in Luke 22:14–20—we emphasize the words that it has in common with Paul:

> And when the hour came, He sat at table, and the apostles with Him.
> And He said to them, "I have earnestly desired to eat this Passover
> with you before I suffer; for I tell you I shall not eat it until it is

fulfilled in the kingdom of God." And He took a cup, and when He had given thanks He said, "Take this, and divide it among yourselves; for I tell you that from now on I shall not drink of the fruit of the vine until the kingdom of God comes." And *He took bread, gave thanks, broke it* and gave it to them, *and said, "This is My body* (given *for you. Do this in remembrance of Me." And the cup in the same way, after the meal, with the words: "This cup is the new covenant in My blood,* poured out for you).

The written tradition represented by Mark and Paul clearly lay before the author of this text and served as sources. The text, however, is not simply a combination of the two. Besides what is taken over from Mark (for example, the "poured out for . . ." in Luke 22:20 in comparison with Mark 14:24) and Paul, Luke contains some remarkable peculiarities in verses 15–18, of which the most striking is the blessing and the distribution of a cup before the bread. So the Lucan account, as we read it, has two cups. What is said of the fruit of the vine, which follows what is said of the cup in Mark, here is put after the distribution of the first cup. Before this in verse 15 we have a word about "this Passover" and the fulfillment in the kingdom of God.

Even if the manuscript transmission were completely consistent, one would have to ask—above all because of the two cups—whether the text is completely in order. However, verses 19b and 20, in parentheses in our translation above, are missing in the old Latin and Syrian manuscripts, as also in the Greek Codex D. Not only such a careful textual critic and exegete as Theodor Zahn but also almost all English theology and today indeed also the overwhelming majority of German theologians have decided in this case that the manuscripts just named have preserved the authentic text of Luke in contrast to the mass of the Greek codices, that therefore vv. 19b–20 did not belong to the original body of the Third Gospel. In fact, the addition of these words, which are clearly borrowed from the Pauline account of the Lord's Supper, may be easier to understand than their omission. Zahn (*Das Evangelium des Lukas* [1913], 678f.) has taken the view—and Jeremias (*Abendmahlsworte*, 44ff. [*Eucharistic Words*, 158f.]) has recently supported this view with very impressive reasons—that Luke could only write about the Last Supper in an incomplete and unclear way in view of Theophilus and other readers like him who had not yet been received into the congregation, because of the calumnies to which the celebration of the Lord's Supper was exposed. That certainly contains an accurate observation. Already in the period of the New Testament, long before the

55

later discipline of secrecy was taught in the church, one clearly avoided saying more about the Lord's Supper in public than was absolutely necessary. The silence of John's gospel regarding the institution of the Lord's Supper, the absence of the Lord's Supper in the list of subjects that belong to elementary instruction in the church according to Hebrews 6:1f., and many other examples speak for the correctness of the thesis recently substantiated anew by Jeremias with great insight and much new material. If the shorter reading is the genuine one, there is hardly a more plausible explanation than this, and we would then have to put up with the fact that Luke gives the decisive words of the Lord's Supper, "This is My body," without any veil or circumlocution but lets them stand in their total starkness as a puzzle for the world.

But does the manuscript evidence really require that preference be given to Codex D, which is otherwise never regarded as primary? Isn't the deletion of 19b–20 perhaps just one of the manifold attempts particularly evident in the variants of the Syrian manuscripts to remove the problem that the apparent doubling of the cup at the Last Supper in Luke causes? (Details about the objections to the shorter text are found in E. Lohmeyer, *Theol. Rundschau*, New Series, 9 [1937]: 178ff.; A. Arnold, *Der Ursprung des christlichen Abendmahls* [1937], 31ff., where it is pointed out that Tatian, from whom the most important variants of D seem to come, knows v. 20.) We can scarcely agree with Zahn that if the longer reading were the original one, it would give rise to no questions or changes. Then we would at best expect that not the second but the first cup would be deleted. If 19b and 20 are an insertion, then it is indeed a very old one, for Marcion (Marcion omits "new" before "covenant" in Luke 22:20) and Justin (Justin names as his source "the recollections of the apostles," i. e., the gospels [*Ap.* 1. 66. 3; 67. 3]. His text therefore depends on Luke, not on Paul.) already know no other than the longer reading.

Since the question of the authenticity of Luke 22:19b–20 cannot be clearly settled on the basis of the manuscript evidence, we shall consider both possibilities and ask in each of the two cases what the peculiar character of the Lucan account of the Last Supper might be—we have already described its external peculiarities, the most important of which were the differences from Paul and Mark.

Common to both forms of the text, that from D and that from the *textus receptus*, is the stronger emphasis on the eschatological character of the Lord's Supper and its connection with the Passover. In doing this the tradition represented by Luke brings nothing fundamentally new, for neither Mark (14:25) nor Paul (1 Cor. 11:26) lacks their respective views of the messianic banquet and Christ's return. Both know of the connection between the Last Supper and the Passover (Mark 14:12–16; 1 Cor. 5:7ff.) What is peculiar to Luke's longer text is that he combines this eschatological outlook with the Passover, which precedes the actual Lord's Supper, and has the word about the fruit of the vine, which in Mark follows the word about the cup, spoken at the distribution of a cup that is not yet the cup of the Lord's Supper but can only be one of the cups passed in the Passover (as Procksch points out ["Passa und Abendmahl" in *Vom Sakrament des Altars*, ed. Hermann Sasse (Leipzig, 1941)], 20). The understanding of the Lord's Supper itself in the longer Lucan text is exactly the same as in Paul.

In the case of the shorter reading it appears to be otherwise. If we had no other account of the origin and essence of the early Christian Lord's Supper, we would have to assume that Jesus gave His disciples first the cup and then the bread. With the cup He spoke eschatologically of the fruit of the vine. With the bread He spoke the puzzling words of explanation, "This is My body," in isolation.

If we take this reading to be the original, we have to ask why Luke portrayed the event in this way. Does he do it because he regards the traditions of Paul and Mark, which he has before him, as false and wants to replace them with a better one? That is altogether unlikely. Then the only explanation we have is that his report does not seek to describe the institution of the Lord's Supper but only to allude to it. So he hides the cup of the Lord's Supper with its word about the blood of the covenant behind the cup of blessing of the Passover meal with its eschatological word. For the same reason then he breaks off the words of the Lord's Supper with "This is My body," leaving the explanation in the dark.

Justin proceeded in a similar way when he felt compelled to confront the slanders of the heathen with some authentic facts of the Lord's Supper. The apostles, as he tells it in *Ap.* 1. 66, report "that the following instruction was given to them. Jesus took bread, spoke a prayer of thanksgiving, and said, 'This do in remembrance of Me; this is My body,' and in the same way He took the cup, spoke a prayer of thanksgiving, and said, 'This is My blood.' " The transposition of the command to repeat and the abbreviation of the words of explanation show how the apologist was concerned not to reveal the secret completely. One does not say it all, and one at least alters the sequence if one has to speak. (That probably also explains the vague rendering of the Rule of Faith in Irenaeus and Tertullian. There too, where the content must be disclosed, the exact wording is not given. The same predicament, having to impart the holy teaching to someone else and yet being obliged to conceal it in essential matters, is found in ancient Buddhism. There too one is helped by regarding only the *literal* reporting of certain teachings as forbidden; see H. Oldenberg, *Buddha*, 8th and 9th edition [1921], 418f.) Therefore, in the shorter reading of Luke the Passover cup serves to point to the cup of the Lord's Supper and at the same time to conceal it. The reversal of the sequence of bread and cup that then results is a welcome means of veiling what actually happened. This raises the possibility that a liturgical custom in the *Didache* and perhaps already hinted at in 1 Cor. 10:16 and 21, in which the Eucharistic prayer over the cup is spoken before the Eucharistic prayer over the bread, may reflect the cup-bread sequence of the shorter Lucan reading. One may not, however, regard the traces of such a usage as proof of the historical reliability of this reading. For the very writings in which they may be found testify quite unmistakably that in the *participation* in the Lord's Supper the bread precedes the cup. (According to *Didache* 9. [5.] the prayer of thanksgiving is first spoken for the cup, then for the bread, but in the instruction it always speaks of the "eating and drinking" of the Eucharist, and the concluding prayer at 10. 3. refers to "food and drink," "spiritual food and drink." Also in Paul at 1 Cor. 10:16f.—the reference shows close connections with *Didache* 9. 4. and 10. 5.—first "the cup which we bless" and then "the bread which we break" are mentioned. That one cannot draw too far-reaching conclusions for practical use from this sequence, which in 10:21 is even used of eating and drinking, is seen by 1 Cor. 11:23–26.)

Therefore even the shorter reading in Luke testifies of no other Lord's Supper than that we know from Paul and Mark. Even someone who cannot accept the view that Luke wanted to veil what actually happened at the institution and who sees in the variations of the shorter reading a conscious correction of the other traditions is still not able to wring another meaning of the Lord's Supper from this reading. One cannot say that Luke pictures a Lord's Supper that is not an explanation and appropriation of the death of Christ but only an anticipation of the messianic banquet. For the connection both with the messianic banquet in the kingdom of God and with the death of Jesus belongs to every tradition of the Lord's Supper, even though sometimes the one, sometimes the other may be more prominent. The absence of the word about the blood of the covenant does not by itself alter the character of the

Lord's Supper. As long as the words "This is My body" are there, the account in Luke, where his own peculiarity may always remain, shares what is essential with Mark and Paul.

Some scholars, like Bultmann (*Jesus*, 30), K. L. Schmidt (*RGG*[2] 1:8), and for a time Lietzmann (*1 Cor.*[2], Handbuch zum N. T., 60; otherwise in *Messe und Herrenmahl*, 216), have gone a step further and have excised also v. 19a from the older account of the Lord's Supper as it is contained in Luke's gospel. But an operation like the deletion of 19a lacks justification either in textual criticism or in literary criticism. It is purely the product of the prejudice that the Lucan text must provide an older account of Jesus' Last Supper, one different from Mark and Paul. But is it any wonder that the Lucan account differs completely from the others if one declares that what he has in common with them is inauthentic? "What remains by this time describes how Jesus at His last meal in the circle of His disciples expressed the conviction that He would celebrate His next meal with His own in the kingdom of God" (K. L. Schmidt, *RGG*[2] 1:8). That is indeed all that remains if one has removed everything else. P. Feine is not unfair when he observes that with this method he could prove anything.

The voices that declare 19a inauthentic are heard less and less. Nevertheless, the efforts to discover in Luke's shorter reading the desired tradition about the Lord's Supper different from Mark and Paul have not ceased. Lietzmann (*Messe und Herrenmahl*, 218) finds "that Luke describes a Lord's Supper that contains eschatological hopes, and in which the bread is the essential feature" [*Mass and Lord's Supper*, 176]. But he is not able to explain the words, "This is My body." They form the strongest objection to his conjecture that the oldest, pre-Pauline Lord's Supper was only the continuation of the table fellowship that Jesus had with His disciples while on earth and of its customary breaking of bread. Lietzmann's hypothesis becomes no more acceptable by his pointing to the breaking of bread in the Emmaus pericope and in Acts. For neither the name "breaking of bread" nor the observation that the celebration was held with "gladness" permit the conclusion that there is something essentially different going on than in the Lord's Supper in the Pauline congregations. Also the absence of the reference to the death of Christ in the prayers of the *Didache* does not prove that the remembrance of the death of Jesus was lacking in this Eucharist. We could only say that if we had the complete liturgy of the church out of which the *Didache* comes. As long as the statement "This is My body" must hold good as an authentic word of Jesus, which also played a role already in the breaking of bread in the early church, we must assume that there has never been a Lord's Supper that was not also a memorial celebration of the death of Jesus and a repetition of His Last Supper.

An understanding of the Lord's Supper different from that in Mark and Paul could only be wrung from Luke's shorter account if it could be shown that the words "This is My body" have a different meaning for him than for Paul and Mark. This is what Rudolf Otto (*Reich Gottes und Menschensohn*, 2d ed. [1940], 214ff.) has tried to prove. He believes that he has discovered the oldest account of the Lord's Supper in Luke 22:17–19a and 29f. By his joining 29 to 19a, it reads: "This is my body (= this is I myself); and I appoint unto you in covenant the kingdom, as my Father has appointed it unto me in covenant, that you may eat and drink at my table in my kingdom, and sit upon thrones, judging the twelve tribes in Israel" (*Reich Gottes*, 216 [*Kingdom of God and Son of Man* (1943), 274]) But that is an arbitrary combination, and that it is untenable becomes clear from the fact that verses 28–30 are demonstrably put into the context of the account of the Lord's Supper for the first time by Luke, as is also what precedes them. (Luke includes sayings at 22:28ff. that he omitted at 18:23f., as is shown by the parallels at Matt. 19:28f. See A. Arnold, 42). Also untenable is Otto's further assumption that the words "This is My body," in Aramaic *den hu gufi*, should mean nothing more than "This is I Myself." This supposition rests on another, that the words with the cup can under no circumstances come from Jesus and that the later addition of "This is My blood of the covenant" completely changed the original meaning of "body," in the sense that only through the juxtaposition of "body" and "blood" did the word *body* receive the meaning of a physical body. But there is not the slightest clue that such a drastic change in the meaning of "This is my body" ever happened. It would have had to have taken place already in the very earliest period of the church, even before the traditions represented by Paul and Mark were formed, and therefore already during the lifetimes of the eye- and earwitnesses of Jesus' Last Supper. Such an unlikely assumption must rest on firmer ground than what apparently forms its only foundation, namely, the presupposition that the original Lucan account *must* have known a Lord's Supper entirely different than the traditions lying before Paul and Mark. In fact such an older tradition, which differed from the other accounts not only in details but in its basic understanding of the Lord's Supper, cannot be demonstrated. Luke's particular treasure does indeed furnish us with an important supplement to what is reported in Paul and Mark, but precisely not in reference to what these two tell of the actual institution of the Lord's Supper and of the words that Jesus spoke. Therefore, according to all the rules of historical research the traditions contained in Paul and Mark remain the oldest historical source.

Jesus' Last Supper

Whoever tries, on the basis of the sources just discussed, to portray what happened at Jesus' Last Supper, which the church from the earliest days has understood as the institution of the Lord's Supper, must be aware from the start of the limitations of this effort. The more reliable these earliest sources appear to be, the more the historian must be on his guard against reading more out of them than they say. It is just the nature of the New Testament tradition to display an extraordinary conciseness. The evangelists report what it seemed necessary for their first readers to know and not a word more. For the modern historian this means that he faces regrettable gaps in the tradition; that applies also to the tradition regarding the institution of the Lord's Supper. We cannot reconstruct the "night when He was betrayed" in all details, nor do we know all that went on at the Last Supper. Under these circumstances the task of the historian cannot be the hypothetical reconstruction of what we are not told but only the analysis of what has been handed down for its authenticity and its meaning. This excludes in particular every attempt to establish by way of psychological considerations what was going on in the soul of Jesus at the time of the Last Supper and what He therefore might have said and what He might have meant with His words.

There ought to be an end, once and for all, to such suppositions as those with which Heitmüller (*Taufe und Abendmahl im Urchristentum* [1911], 55f.) tries to clarify the situation in which Jesus spoke the words of the Last Supper (emphasis mine):

> The thought of a catastrophe *must* have stirred in His soul . . . considerations of what would become of His work, of what His life had labored for, of His disciples in case of His death—the struggle for faith itself, for His work, for His God. On the evening before His arrest, *presentiment* would become, if not *knowledge*, then surely *certainty*. This is *psychologically understandable*. This acceptance is supported by His word: "From now on I shall not drink of the fruit . . . ." A *mood* of farewell moves Him. Thoughts of death fill His soul. As He reclined with His own for the meal, He was sure that this was the last fraternal meal. All His thoughts about this termination of His

work *closed in* on Him again; all love for His disciples intensified vividly. He is not defeated in His struggle for faith in His God and His work. He is sure in the joyful hope that some day He would be united again with His own in the Father's kingdom. But what would become of the flock of those who were His, whose faith and weaknesses he knew so well . . . ?"

Just as untenable is what we read in Dalman (*Jesus-Jeschua* [1922], 131f.; emphasis mine):

On this night He performed the breaking of bread, certain of His approaching death, His soul full of the destiny that His Father had designed for Him. How *natural* it was, as He set about breaking and distributing the bread piece by piece, that *the thought pierced His soul:* "This is what will happen to Me when I have to suffer death."

The text does not offer the slightest clue for such constructions, in which the exegesis of rationalism still lingers. (Cf. the interpretation of H. G. E. Paulus in 1805: "The breaking of the bread caught the mind of Jesus, filled with thoughts of death, by surprise for a moment over the similarity to a murderous dismemberment. The sight of the grapes' blood convulsed Jesus: This is to Me suddenly like My own blood" [quoted by Herman Schultz, *Zur Lehre vom Heiligen Abendmahl* (1886), 8].) They serve not to explain but to obscure the actual situation, for they squeeze the Lord, who is instituting His Supper, into the psychological categories of modern Western man.

An explicit warning about this wrong track is therefore necessary at this point because numerous interpreters of the Lord's Supper pericope have let themselves be led astray by such psychologizing tendencies. The more "naturally," the more self-evidently an exegete fits the celebration of the Last Supper into the whole life of Jesus as a farewell meal and legacy and the more this celebration has forfeited the character of the surprising, the extraordinary, and the offensive, then the more necessary it is for concerned exegesis to examine whether it has fallen victim to that danger of psychologizing. It is not historical interpretation of the pericope of the Last Supper if a historian tells us what his thoughts would have been, had he been there speaking the Words of Institution. To interpret this pericope does not mean to paint moods—neither Jesus' mood nor the mood of His disciples—nor does it mean to guess at thoughts that might have "closed in" on Jesus at that time or "pierced His soul." It means to give an account soberly and objectively of what *happened*, what was *said*, and what was *meant* by the words.

So what did happen then? Jesus sat down, or more precisely, He reclined—as was the custom at the Passover meal—at table with His disciples. The first Lord's Supper took place during a meal, and this combination of the Lord's Supper with a meal was maintained for a considerable time, as we know, in the agape meals of the early Christians. Only in the middle of the second century does Justin tell us that in Rome at that time the Lord's Supper was separated from the usual time for the meal and transferred to the divine service on Sunday morning. From this combination of the Lord's Supper with a regular meal, however, it cannot be concluded that Jesus' last meal was only an ordinary meal and not a Passover meal. The meal that Jesus as head of the house [*Hausvater*] had that night with His circle of disciples was much more. It was indeed a farewell meal, a last time of fellowship at table together. It was also a Passover meal, whether one understands it with the Eastern tradition and such modern scholars as O. Procksch as an anticipated celebration or with the Western church and many recent theologians as an actual Passover meal. These alternatives may perhaps never be resolved with complete certainty, but the fact that Jesus Himself understood the meal as a Passover meal should never be disputed. Jeremias has shown how Jesus' last meal in all details fits into the framework of a Passover meal. The only remaining counter-argument is the difficult problem of the date. Was the Thursday on which the Passover was eaten Nisan 14, and was Jesus executed on the first day of the high feast? Is an anticipated Passover, a Passover without a Passover lamb, on the day before Nisan 14 conceivable? However one may answer these questions, it is impossible to undo the connection between Jesus' last meal and the Passover meal without doing violence to the reports. The account of the preparation for the Passover (Mark 14:12–16 and parallels)—"one of the most beautiful in the Gospel of Mark" (E. Lohmeyer, *Das Evangelium des Markus* [1937], 298)—is utterly credible and with its local color and vividness offers no ground for critical doubt. So strong is its connection with the pericope of the Last Supper that it can only be broken by force. Even if the institution pericope can be interpreted without the report of the preparations (e. g., 1 Cor. 11), the latter only has its culmination in the former and never existed for itself alone.

In the course of this Passover meal then there occurred what Mark 14:22f. describes with the words: "And as they were eating, He took bread, and blessed, and broke it, and gave it to them and said, 'Take; this is My body.' And He took a cup, gave thanks, and gave it them, and they all drank of it. And He said to them, 'This is My blood of the covenant, which is poured out for many' " [14:22–24]. The exact moment of this action or these two actions cannot be determined with certainty. According to Mark the distribution of the cup seems to follow immediately that of the bread. According to the tradition preserved in Paul ("after supper," 1 Cor. 11:25), two things were done, of which the second, the distribution of the blessed cup, took place at the end of the meal, while the first came earlier, either at the beginning of the meal or during it. Jeremias (*Abendmahlsworte*, 41 [*Eucharistic Words*, 87]) and Billerbeck (Strack-Billerbeck, *Kommentar zum N. T. aus Talmud und Midrasch* 4:75) take the view that Jesus attached His words about the bread and wine to the table prayer that the head of the house spoke over the unleavened bread immediately before the eating of the Passover lamb and to the prayer of thanksgiving that was spoken over the "third" cup, "the cup of blessing" (1 Cor. 10:16), at the end of the actual meal before the "hymn of praise" (Mark 14:26, the Passover Hallel). This is very likely. That the connection between the first Lord's Supper and the Passover liturgy is not more clearly expressed in the accounts that we have may be reasonably explained by the fact that these traditions have been influenced by the liturgical interests of the early church. The ecclesiastical traditions had no further interest in the details of the Passover ritual. Its whole attention was concentrated on what has remained in the liturgy of the church from the first Lord's Supper (Arnold, 77f.). This also explains why in the Marcan account there is not even a hint of what went on between the distribution of the bread and the cup. That, along with all the details of the traditional Passover ritual, which Jesus doubtless observed, was irrelevant for the Lord's Supper itself. Where the Passover of the New Testament is celebrated, that of the Old Testament is both fulfilled and abolished. The early church had already perceived what was later put into words: "This new Passover's new blessing Hath fulfilled the older rite" (So Thomas Aquinas in "Lauda Sion salvatorem." Among the church fathers the thought is found in Athanasius, Ephraem Syrus, Chrysostom, Theodoret of Cyrrhus, and Peter of Laodicea, among others; cf. O. Casel, *Das Mysterien-Gedächtnis der Messliturgie*, 148, 151, 153, 155, 158.)

Jesus performed two actions during the meal: the blessing, breaking, and distributing of the bread and the blessing and distribution of the cup. Both actions belong as such to the settled way of Jewish religious table customs, and they occur not only in the Passover celebration but also at other meals, such as at the family meal with which the celebration of the Sabbath begins on Friday evening. Also of Jesus is the "He took bread, gave thanks, and broke it" attested not only at the Last Supper but also at the miraculous feeding and in the Emmaus story, which appears to allude to the breaking of bread that He practiced during His days on earth. The praise of God the Creator for the bread, the grateful recall of the blessings that God has heaped on His people, the breaking of the bread and its distribution to those taking part in the meal as a sign of their participation in the praise, the prayer of thanksgiving over the cup, and perhaps also its distribution—these are all Jewish customs practiced by Jesus in harmony with the piety of His people. They supply the ingredients of the action that He performed at the Last Supper, and that is different from similar actions in that He Himself did not partake of the bread and the wine as the head of the family usually did. That can at least explain the invitation, "Take," in Mark 14:22. (The "Take" is not there in Luke and Paul—in Matthew it is expanded to "Take, eat . . . drink." The *labete* may be compared with the inscription *labe eulogia* on a Jewish gold-ornamented glass cup; cf. Lietzmann, *Messe und Abendmahl*, 209 [*Mass and Lord's Supper*, 169f.].) But regardless of how much His action may resemble Jewish benediction rites, it can scarcely be derived from them. It is not what the action of Jesus on that night has in common with these rites that gives the Lord's Supper its character, but what distinguishes it from them. Just as the early Christian agape meals appeared externally to be interchangeable with the Jewish fellowship meals and yet according to their inner meaning were something quite new, so is it with the blessing and distribution of bread and wine at Jesus' Last Supper. What happened there was something quite new, a special action that receives its meaning only from the words that He spoke along with it.

The *words of explanation* with which Jesus accompanied His action are therefore the key to understanding the Lord's Supper. They reveal the difference between His action and that of a pious Jewish head of the house who eats the Passover with his family and speaks the traditional blessings. They not only distinguish the Lord's Supper from the Passover, but also this Last Supper of Jesus from all the meals that He had had with His disciples before. The assertion has been made that the earliest Lord's Supper of the church, "the breaking of bread" of the original Jerusalem congregation, is not to be understood as a repetition of Jesus' Last Supper at all, but as a continuation of the table fellowship that He had always had with His disciples. There is a kernel of truth in this hypothesis. In fact, there must have been something special in the table fellowship between Jesus and His disciples even before and apart from the Last Supper. The "breaking of bread" does indeed go back to Jesus' days on earth. It was performed by Jesus daily as the action of blessing before their common meals, and once, at the feeding of the five thousand, it occurred before a great many people. This "breaking of bread" that Jesus performed in the circle of His disciples lives on in the Lord's Supper of the early church. That is the element of truth in Lietzmann's thesis about the origin of the Lord's Supper. Its error lies in the fact that it does not perceive what Jesus' Last Supper means in this context. While it is the end, the culmination of the breaking of bread performed by Jesus Himself, it is also the beginning of a new celebration in which Jesus' breaking of bread was "lifted up," the celebration of a much closer fellowship than the earthly table fellowship had been. In this celebration the Lord is not only a table companion, not only the host who speaks the blessing, not only the head of the house who eats the Passover with His own, but He is Himself also the food and drink of the meal. He is the Passover lamb, the sacrificial food that is eaten, His blood the holy drink that is drunk. Thus in this meal a fellowship is established in which the old table fellowship lives on and which at the same time is a much closer and deeper fellowship. There is no analogy to this fellowship, just as there are also no parallels to this celebration. The Lord's Supper received this character as something unique, something remarkable from the Words of Institution.

The Words of Institution

We have already observed the notable fact that the Words of Institution—just like the Lord's Prayer—have not been entirely uniformly transmitted (how this diversity is to be judged in the light of the history of the liturgy is shown in the work of F. Hamm cited above), but at the same time we have established that the forms of the text essentially agree and that the original form of the words is still recognizable. Since Matthew gives the Marcan form with the addition of "for the forgiveness of sins" to the words about the cup, and since the longer Lucan text is dependent on Paul, the original form of the words of the Lord's Supper must be ascertained from a comparison of Mark and Paul. This comparison shows that the Marcan form of the text is older than the Pauline, in which the words about the cup have been touched up, and the command to repeat has been added to both of the words of explanation. We agree with Jeremias, who expresses the result of his careful examination of the Words of Institution as follows: "The oldest text of the words of interpretation obtained by a comparison of the texts agrees exactly with the Marcan text" (*Abendmahlsworte* [1935], 64 [Cf. *Eucharistic Words*, 173]). This text reads: *labete touto estin to sōma mou . . . touto estin to haima mou tēs diathēkēs to ekchunnomenon huper pollōn*. "Take! This is My body. . . . This is My covenant blood poured out for many."

What do these words, the most disputed in the New Testament, mean? We are assured that "today there is agreement from Zürich to Erlangen . . . that the decisive texts of the Lord's Supper are to be understood symbolically" (W. Niesel, *Abendmahlsgemeinschaft?* [1937], 37), and this assertion is supported by pointing to the more recent exegesis, which has shown that the words of the Lord's Supper have a parabolic character. If this is in fact an assured result of more recent research, then we would expect that these exegetes would have arrived at a consensus on what this parable should mean. But that is by no means the case.

Jülicher, the founder of the theory that the words of the Lord's Supper are a double parable comparable to the double parables of mustard seed and leaven, the lost sheep and coin, and others, understands the meaning of "This is My body" as follows:

> At the breaking of the bread into pieces He thought of the similar fate that awaited His body, and with no other perception of profound similarities between His body and the bread than what was there before His eyes, He could in view of the *klōmenon* before Him say to His disciples: This is My body; this same treatment will presently happen to My body. This they could all understand. . . . He was describing what His body would suffer, not what the disciples should do." (Ad. Jülicher, "Zur Geschichte der Abendmahlsfeier," *Theol. Abhandlg. C. v. Weizsäcker gewidmet* [1892], 242f.)

The point of comparison here is the being broken in pieces and then also the being poured out (Ibid., 244). Heitmüller (*Taufe und Abendmahl im Urchristentum* [1911], 57) objects that this symbolism may hold for the bread, but not for the cup, of whose pouring out or consumption nothing is said. Jülicher's interpretation has forgotten that bread and wine are distributed in order to be eaten and drunk:

> In view of this another interpretation may here be proposed . . . :
> "Just as I give all of you this one bread and you all eat of the one bread as the sign and as the foundation of a closer fellowship, so do I give you My body, that is, Me Myself, and so you are to receive Me

into yourselves as the resource for a most intimate brotherhood and fellowship." (Ibid., 58)

Here the point of comparison is in having a part in the one gift. Althaus interprets the action of the Lord at the Last Supper still differently:

> The action is first of all Jesus' last parable: He proclaims by means of a symbol together with the interpreting words His imminent death. By making the bread and wine into symbols of His sacrificial death, He portrays the meaning of His death for the life of men: "You live because I die."

The action is both "parabolic action" [*Gleichnishandlung*] and a "done parable [*Tatgleichnis*], that is, a real gift in symbolic action" (*Die luth. Abendmahlslehre in der Gegenwart* [1931], 43f.). For Althaus the point of comparison is separate handing over of the bread and wine as symbols of body and blood: "Only in death are body and blood separated. Jesus therefore points in the symbolic action to His sacrificial death. In going to His death He gives up His life for the disciples" (Ibid., 39). "The gift of the Sacrament is therefore not Christ's heavenly corporeality, but His death" (*Grundriss der Dogmatik*, part 2 [1932], 152). Lietzmann has greater difficulty in finding the point of comparison:

> A distinct problem is posed by the question: How can Jesus compare the bread to his body and the wine to his blood in a context of this kind? Where is the third term of comparison? The early comment that the breaking of the bread into pieces is a symbol of the dismembered body of the victim is obvious enough; but it is difficult to find an analogous point of comparison in the case of the wine. It is true that it is "poured out"—from the pitcher into the cup, from the cup into the throat—but everyone feels that this figure is less appropriate: the pouring out from the pitcher probably took place before Jesus spoke. . . . It is easy to see the bread as a symbol of Jesus dying as a victim for his people; this is not so in the case of the wine, yet it is the words connected in the tradition with the wine which have compelled us to adopt the dominant conception of the victim and his blood-covenant; and it is only by starting from this conception that we have come to our interpretation of the words concerning the bread. (*Messe und Herrenmahl*, 221f. [*Mass and Lord's Supper*, 180–81])

Jeremias finds it easier to explain the "double parable." After he correctly points out that *touto* cannot possibly refer to the action of breaking or the action of pouring out, since the words of explanation were not spoken until long after the actions, he states:

It was not the action of breaking the bread or of pouring out the wine that Jesus interpreted, but rather the bread and wine itself. . . . The *tertium comparationis* in the case of the bread is the fact that it was broken, and in the case of the wine the red color. . . . Jesus made the broken bread a simile of the fate of his body, the blood of the grapes a simile of his outpoured blood. "I go to death as the true passover sacrifice," is the meaning of Jesus' last parable. (*Die Abendmahlsworte Jesu* [1935], 75f. [*Eucharistic Words*, 221, 223–24]. That this death is for the benefit of others lies, according to Jeremias, not yet in the parable but in the direct statement about the meaning of His death that is added to the word about the wine [*Abendmahlsworte*, 77 (*Eucharistic Words*, 225)].)

Enough of these examples, which could be multiplied as much as you like! They show that there has been no success so far in explaining the alleged parable in the words of the Lord's Supper. The exegetes indeed assure us: "Its meaning is quite simple. Each one of the disciples could understand it" (Jeremias, *Abendmahlsworte*, 76 [*Eucharistic Words*, 224]; similarly Jülicher, 243), yet they themselves quite clearly cannot agree what that meaning should be. In fact symbolic exegesis today does not seem to have gotten beyond the situation of the 16th century, when Luther again and again had to point out that his opponents were united in only one thing: *that* the words of the Lord's Supper were to be understood symbolically, while they differed widely on the interpretation itself. What sort of a parable can it be when even learned exegetes cannot say with certainty what it actually means!

Let us suppose that after the church for so many centuries has falsely understood the words of the Lord's Supper, at least one of the modern scholars has finally succeeded in discovering their meaning. What sort of meaning would it be? "I must die" is according to Jeremias "the meaning of Jesus' last parable"; according to Althaus (*Abendmahlslehre*, 43): "You live because I die." It is difficult then to see what need there is of the Lord's Supper, for Jesus had already told His disciples that before. Had He wanted to say it once more with special emphasis in His departing hour, wouldn't a direct instruction about the imminent fulfillment of Isaiah 53 have been much more suitable than a parable about whose meaning scholars cannot agree even after 19 centuries? One could respond to this with Althaus that the Last Supper was certainly more than a parable: "In making the bread and the wine into symbols of His death and giving them to be consumed, Jesus was at the same time granting in parabolic pledges a participation in what

His death achieved" (Ibid., 43). Certainly, but all notable representatives of the symbolic interpretation of the words of the Lord's Supper have taught this, even Berengar, Zwingli, and Oecolampadius. For none of them was the Lord's Supper *only* a parable. But it might be asked whether an application of that kind might not have been much more impressive if Jesus had used a plain, straightforward statement of what He was giving His disciples, rather than an ambiguous parable.

But perhaps He did that! Perhaps His words are to be taken quite literally, just as they read! If that should be the case, then it would certainly be comprehensible that the exegetes have so far not arrived at a unanimous interpretation of the parable presumed to be in the words of the Lord's Supper. How can one explain a parable that is not a parable at all! Perhaps this failure of recent exegesis may serve to shake the dogma held with an astonishing lack of critical thought in modern Protestantism that *touto estin to sōma mou* cannot mean anything but "This *signifies* My body," especially since the copula "is" probably was not even expressed in Aramaic.

It was certainly not just a more or less respectable dogmatic stubbornness, as is supposed today, that caused Luther so decisively to offer resistance to Zwingli's understanding of the *est* as *significat*. It was also good philological reasons. It was also his superlative sensitivity to language and style, in which the greatest Bible translator that Christianity has produced far surpassed his Humanistic contemporaries.

Let us now ask once how Jesus would have expressed Himself if He had intended a parable. Lohmeyer observes, in commenting on Jeremias's attempt to understand the statements as a double parable:

> Linguistically it would have to say *homoion esti to sōma mou toutō* or something similar to *homoia estin hē basileia tōn ouranōn zumē.* Also the reference to the word of explanation with the unleavened bread [*Mazzot*], "This is the bread of affliction," proves nothing. For there a comparison is clearly indicated by the repetition of the word "bread," and this repetition is just what is altogether absent in Jesus' word. (*Das Evangelium des Markus* [1937], 306 n. 2)

No help is given here either by reference to such expressions as "I am the Bread of life," "I am the true Vine," or "I am the Good Shepherd," for in these expressions the "I am" does not at all mean "I signify." No one denies that *esti* can also be used in the sense of "signifies," but in that case the comparison must be recognizable as a comparison. That applies also to a parabolic action. Thus Agabus in Acts 21:11 makes it clear that he has acted parabolically with the words: "So shall the Jews at Jerusalem bind the man who owns this girdle and deliver him into the hands of the Gentiles." Similar explanations are given of parabolic actions in Jer. 19:19ff. and Ezek. 4:1ff.; 5:1ff. (One notes the "Thus . . . . So" in Jer. 19:11 and the continuation "This is Jerusalem" in Ezek. 5:5ff.)

To understand the action and the words of the Lord's Supper as a parable is linguistically impossible. Wherever it has been tried, it has not happened for philological reasons, but—and this ought to be freely acknowledged—only from the consideration that if the Words of Institution are taken literally, they appear to state something absurd.

The words of the Lord's Supper do in fact appear to express an absurdity if one understands them literally. How can Jesus say that the bread that He holds in His hand, that He breaks and distributes, is His body, that the wine in the cup is His blood? And if He actually meant that, how could the disciples understand it? "How could Jesus give His glorified body to His disciples while He was still corporeally sitting in front of them and the glorification was still to come? . . . But above all: The disciples absolutely could not have been able to understand this word in this sense. Yet Jesus certainly did not offer them a riddle in this solemn moment" (Heitmüller, 56f.). But if, as we saw, the words of the Lord's Supper become an insoluble riddle if one tries to interpret them as a parable, how then are we to escape the absurdity? It can be done if one accepts that Jesus gave His disciples "body" and "blood" not figuratively but actually, but that the words "body" and "blood" do not mean what we in our language call "body" and "blood." And so the understanding of "body" in the sense of "person" enjoys great popularity in our day. If "This is My body" is put into Aramaic as *den hu gufi*, as is generally accepted today, then one easily understands *gufi*, "My body," in the sense in which it is often used, namely, for "I myself." (Similarly Kattenbusch, who takes *gewijjah* as the basis for "My body": "With Jesus 'my body' means 'I' " ["Der Quellort der Kirchenidee" in *Festgabe für A. von Harnack* (1921), 170 n. 1].) In a careful discussion of this question, Dalman comes to the conclusion: "It would be possible to take *guphi* in the sense of 'I myself.' However, the fact that the Early Christians did not take it in this sense, as well as our Lord's reference to His Blood at the administration of the wine, necessitates the translation 'My Body' (G. Dalmann, *Jesus-Jeschua* [1922], 131 [*Jesus-Jeshua*, 143]). In fact this understanding of "My body" would only make sense if one either could find a similar transferred meaning for blood, of which there is none, or if one with R. Otto (*Reich Gottes und Menschensohn*, 2d ed., 214ff. [*The Kingdom of God and the Son of Man*, 320f.]) and his

71

followers (e. g., E. Käsemann, *Abendmahlsgemeinschaft*? 67f.) denies that Jesus spoke the words about the cup at all, which we have seen as impossible in another connection (see on p. 59). If "My blood of the covenant poured out for many" unquestionably means the actual blood of Jesus that was poured out on the cross, then "My body" can only mean His actual body that was given into death.

Another new interpretation of body and blood has recently been proposed by Lohmeyer. He recognizes, as we have already seen, the impossibility of understanding the words of the Lord's Supper as a parable. "Therefore we are not here involved in looking for the third factor by which bread and body can be compared with each other. . . ," but the "supposed identity between bread and body is the riddle and mystery that contains in itself the meaning of the action" (*Das Evangelium des Markus*, 306). In the statements "This is My body" and "This is My covenant blood," "this" must be taken as a predicate noun, not as the subject. These statements do not say what the bread and wine but what the body and blood now are. "Now the bread the disciples take and the wine they drink signify nothing else than the fellowship in fulfillment. Body and blood signify nothing else than the earthly life of this one Master, who is the norm and the fact of their fellowship. Through the idea of fellowship therefore an identity between bread and wine becomes possible" (Ibid., 306f.). The meaning of the action at the Last Supper and the word about the bread is then given as follows: "As My body was the means and the heart of the disciples' fellowship so far, so now it is the common eating of the bread"; to say it on the model of a familiar saying of Jesus: "Where two or three break the bread, there am I in the midst of them."

The word of the covenant blood must then be similarly understood. However cleverly Lohmeyer may carry this theory through, it is simply not tenable. To take *touto* as a predicate noun placed in front of the statement is far too artificial and needs better substantiation in view of the fact that since the early church *touto* has always been understood as subject. It founders in the setting of the word about the cup in 1 Cor. 11:25: *touto potērion hē kainē diathēkē estin en tō emō haimati*, and in Luke 22:20: *touto to potērion hē kainē diathēkē en tō haimati mou*. For here "this cup" without any doubt is understood as subject, and there is not the slightest clue for finding that it was otherwise in Mark or Matthew.

Apart from this question, Lohmeyer's thesis means a new attempt to make the identification of bread and body, wine and blood comprehensible by a new interpretation of "body" and "blood." "Body and blood," according to Lohmeyer, means "nothing else than the earthly life of this one Master," and "My body" means "the person of the Master." He does not investigate the Aramaic background. But what does "My covenant blood" mean? There is nothing said of this with the same clarity. We are told only that the word about the cup says the same as the word about the bread, and the equation of blood and wine means: "That which is the content and power of His life and death now happens in the fellowship of the eating and drinking" (Ibid., 308). So then, there is no actual identity of the bread and the wine with the body and blood of Christ, but a functional identity of both. The bread and the wine or, more precisely, the eating and drinking of the bread and wine now exercise the same function of establishing fellowship that previously Christ's body and blood or, more precisely, His bodily presence and His death exercised: "Whenever, therefore, the disciples break the bread together and drink the wine, this meal brings about the same fellowship, as much historic as eschatological, that was previously embodied in the figure of the Master. To say it more precisely, the fellowship of the brothers that is effected in the eating and drinking is the presence of the Lord" (Ibid.).

But we need only raise the question whether this fellowship, whether this presence of the Lord can not also be mediated in other ways, whether it is not wherever two or three are gathered together in His name to hear His word and to call on Him in prayer, there is He in the midst of them, and we will recognize that there is in this theory no real identification of the bread with the body, the wine with the blood. It fails to explain "the riddle and mystery" of the equation of body and bread, wine and blood; much rather it shatters this identification by its complicated efforts at explanation. For Lohmeyer, too, the bread is not actually the body nor the wine actually the blood of Christ.

There is a still weightier objection to raise against all these attempts at new interpretations. Their advocates can only explain the unquestioned fact that the church has always taken "body" to be the actual body and "blood" to be the actual blood of the Lord in such a way that this ecclesiastical understanding of the words of the Lord's Supper represents either a misunderstanding or a development of the original Lord's Supper. But when could this misunderstanding or this development have occurred? Perhaps first with Ignatius at the beginning or with Justin in the middle of the second century? Is not this realistic understanding of the words of the Lord's Supper found already in Paul, our oldest witness of the Lord's Supper, and in the four gospels? Even those scholars who are of the opinion that Jesus Himself used "body" and "blood" in a transferred sense acknowledge that in places like 1 Cor. 10 and 11 or John 6:51b-58 a realistic understanding of the Words of Institution is taken for granted. This question calls for investigation.

The Understanding of the Words of Institution in Paul and John

In what sense "is" the bread the body and the wine in the cup the blood of Christ for Paul? There is no doubt that according to Paul those who take part in the Lord's Supper actually consume bread and wine. According to 1 Cor. 10:17 they all partake of the *one bread*, and 11:27ff. confirms that the communicants actually consume bread and wine: "Whoever, therefore, eats the bread or drinks the cup of the Lord in an unworthy manner will be guilty of profaning the body and blood of the Lord. Let a man examine himself, and so eat of the bread and drink of the cup." This passage has always been legitimately quoted against the doctrine of transubstantiation (SA III 6). If the bread were *changed* into the body of Christ, it could no longer be designated as the object of the eating. And if Paul meant that it is now only figurative bread, he would express himself differently. But do the communicants receive *only* bread and wine? No, for "the cup of blessing which we bless, is it not a participation [*koinōnia*] in the blood of Christ? The bread which we break, is it not a participation in the body of Christ?" (10:16). "Participation in the body of Christ" may not be taken, as has been attempted, as a figurative expression for the fellowship of the church. In that case, what would "participation in the blood of Christ" be? It really deals, therefore, with a communion with the body given into death "for you" (11:24) and with the blood shed on the cross. Paul chooses the term *koinōnia*, communion; he avoids the word *metechein*, partake, which he uses for the participation in the bread (10:17), and he also does not speak of eating the body and drinking the blood. That these formulations are not accidental but deliberate is shown by 10:20f.: "I do not want you to be partners [*koinōnoi*] with demons. You cannot drink the cup of the Lord and the cup of demons. You cannot partake of the table of the Lord and the table of demons." One drinks the cup, one partakes [*metechein*] at the table, that is, one eats and thereby comes into communion with the demons in the heathen cult, with the body and blood of Christ in the Lord's Supper. The distinction between "partaking" and "com-

74

munion" expresses the distinction that exists in the relationship the communicants have with the bread on the one hand and with the body and blood of Christ on the other hand. In order not to blur this distinction, Paul avoids, probably on purpose, the expressions "eat the body of Christ" and "drink the blood of Christ," which for some reason may have seemed dubious to him. One may certainly not understand this as though the "participation in the body and blood of Christ" is something purely spiritual and not as close and as real as the connection of food and drink to the human body. In the Bible the word *koinōnia* signifies the closest and deepest communion conceivable between God and man (1 John 1:3) and between the members of the body of Christ, a communion in which our body also takes part (1 Cor. 6:15).

It would also be a misinterpretation of Paul to suppose that the koinonia of the body and blood of Christ is established in any other way than by eating the bread and drinking the cup. There is no support in Paul for the notion that the *faith* of the recipient or the *Holy Spirit* brings about the fellowship of the body and blood during the celebration of the Lord's Supper. Nor can one read into 1 Cor. 10:16 the notion that the action of blessing and breaking the bread is what creates the koinonia. (This widespread notion is suggested by the Württemberg Bible Society to the readers of its Bible editions by their emphasizing of the words *bless* and *break* in 1 Cor. 10:16.) It stands there unambiguously: the cup is the koinonia, the bread is the koinonia.

However, from the statement in 1 Cor. 10:16 that the bread is the koinonia of the body, we may not now conclude that the bread is not the body for Paul. Certainly the identity of bread and body may not be understood as if only the bread is the body. Jesus was not saying this when He called the bread He gave His disciples His body, for His body was also beyond the bread. The identity that exists between bread and body is rather to be understood in this way with Jesus as well as with Paul: Where this bread is, there is actually the body of Christ; where this bread is given and received, there the body of Christ is given and received with it. In this sense also for Paul the bread is not only the koinonia of the body, but the body of Christ itself. That follows quite clearly from the continuation in verse 17: "Because there is *one* bread, we who are many are *one* body, for we all partake of the *one* bread." That means: Whoever partakes of the bread has koinonia with the body of Christ, "for Christ's body is that *one* loaf. . . . Christ is so essentially in the elements that, by partaking of them, we incorporate ourselves

75

in him and so become one with him" (H. Lietzmann, *Messe und Herrenmahl*, 224 [*Mass and Lord's Supper*, 182–83]).

The reproach for the unworthy communicant in 11:29 shows that Paul understood the statement in 11:24, "This is My body," literally. The unworthy communicant does not differentiate the Lord's body, which is the only thing it can mean, from ordinary food. But if eating the bread and drinking the cup is what creates the koinonia with the body and blood of Christ, then all who partake of the Lord's Supper come into this "koinonia," both the worthy and the unworthy guests, some blessedly, others the opposite. And of course Paul knows that one cannot speak of a koinonia in the same sense for the unworthy as for the worthy and that one should rather use a different expression for them than koinonia. And he does not use the word *koinonia* in this case. In 10:16f. he is not thinking of the unworthy. The general rule in the New Testament—we observe it also in John—is that the terminology used of the Lord's Supper relates only to the normal situation of worthy reception. As seriously as the church took the problem of Judas's participation in the Last Supper, so clearly has it regarded unworthy reception as the exception, which does not touch the essence of the Sacrament. We may never forget that already in the time of the apostles only the baptized, therefore members of the body of Christ, were admitted to the Lord's Supper as the fellowship of the body and blood of Christ and that already very early we know that an act of confession preceded the celebration (*Didache* 14. 1). *What the Lord's Supper is and what it gives has always been defined on the assumption of worthy and blessed reception.* But when the circumstances in Corinth force the apostle to deal with the question of unworthy participation in the celebration, he leaves no doubt that the unworthy communicants also come into the very closest contact with the body and blood of the Lord, not, however, for their blessing but bringing judgment on themselves. And this judgment expresses itself not in general punishments but in physical consequences: "That is why many of you are weak and ill, and some have died" (11:30). In place of this characteristic formulation one could scarcely put a statement like: "That is why many have not had success in their work, and some have become quite poor." The Lord punishes *physically* those who by unworthy participation in the Lord's Supper are guilty of profaning the body and blood of the Lord. This understanding of 1 Cor. 11:27ff. is confirmed by the statements about the Old Testament types of the Christian sacraments in 10:1ff. Here Paul warns the Corinthians against a false confidence in the supposedly infallible saving power of Baptism and the Lord's Supper:

> I want you to know, brethren, that our fathers were all under the cloud, and all passed through the sea, and all were baptized into Moses in the cloud and in the sea, and all ate the same supernatural food and all drank the same supernatural drink. For they drank from the supernatural Rock which followed them, and the Rock was Christ. Nevertheless with most of them God was not pleased; for they were overthrown in the wilderness.

The parallel is obvious only if, just as once all members of God's people took part in that "baptism" as well as the supernatural food of the manna and the supernatural drink from the supernatural Rock, so now all members of the church, that is, all communicants, consume the supernatural food and the supernatural drink of the Lord's Supper, whether it be for blessing or for judgment. That is the Pauline understanding of the Words of Institution. "It is true," remarks H. Lietzmann (*Messe und Herrenmahl*, 224 [*Mass and Lord's Supper*, 182]) against the attempts of J. Weiss and G. P. Wetter to explain away the identification of "bread" and "body" in 10:17, "that sacramental theology is at variance with the usual tendency to spiritualize on the part of Paul, who is determined not to know anything of flesh and blood but only the risen Lord. But we have to recognize this contradiction and not explain it away."

The realism of the Pauline doctrine of the Lord's Supper is all the more striking as the statements of the apostle are consistently dominated by the unmistakable tendency to prevent any materialistic misunderstanding of the Lord's Supper. This becomes quite clear when we compare his statements with the formulations in the remarkable passage, John 6:51b–58 (on the following see also W. Elert, *Der christliche Glaube*, 458ff. [*The Christian Faith*, 375ff.]). This forms the second part of the long discourse on the bread from heaven, which follows the miracle of the feeding in John. The "bread from heaven"—after the Old Testament expression for manna—in the first part of the discourse, or controversy, that runs through 51a is Jesus Himself: "I am the Bread of life," "I am the living Bread which came down from heaven." To eat this bread, which comes from heaven and gives life to the world (v. 33), means nothing else than to believe in Him. "He who comes to Me shall not hunger, and he who believes in Me shall never thirst" (35). "For this is the will of My Father, that everyone who sees the Son and believes in Him should have eternal life; and I will raise him up at the last day"

(40). This part of the discourse has been properly taken as the scriptural foundation of the doctrine of the *manducatio spiritualis*, the spiritual eating of Christ in faith. But it does violence to the text if one now reads this meaning into the verses from 51b on: "And the bread which I shall give for the life of the world is My flesh. . . . he who eats My flesh and drinks My blood has eternal life, and I will raise him up at the last day. For My flesh is food indeed, and My blood is drink indeed. He who eats My flesh and drinks My blood abides in Me, and I in him. . . . This is the bread which came down from heaven." Here the heavenly bread is no longer the person of Christ but His flesh. Whoever eats the flesh of Christ and drinks His blood is to be raised to eternal life. The transition from one theme to the next is so abrupt, the tension between the statement about the spiritual eating of Christ in faith and that about the sacramental eating and drinking of His flesh and blood is so great that 6:51b–58 has been interpreted as an insertion by which the ecclesiastical doctrine of the Lord's Supper as "medicine of immortality" was introduced into the Fourth Gospel, which was originally not interested in the Sacrament and therefore ignored the institution of the Lord's Supper (thus R. Bultmann, *Das Johannes Evangelium*, 161ff.). Now this gospel, just like the synoptics, also in other respects shows traces of a complicated process of development, and it is quite conceivable that the discourses as we read them today may have come together from various sources. But to lay bare some sort of original John [*Ur-Johannes*] from the text as we have it is impossible. For it has clearly been part of the character of this gospel from the beginning that the parts that seem to contradict each other are fitted together into a whole. Thus 6:51b–58 forms an integrating part of the gospel, and even the tension that exists without a doubt between 6:27–51a and 51b–58 is something that cannot be fancied away. Again and again in the discourses of Jesus in John there are repetitions of a line of thought that at the same time are an extension of it, and an extension in a quite unexpected direction. And much as themes that sound altogether spiritual in the statements about the judgment and the resurrection abruptly stand next to expressions of a massive eschatological realism (John 5:24–29), so here two lines of thought about the bread of life stand next to each other that at first glance seem to contradict each other, and yet for the evangelist they form a contrapuntal pair. Both are true for him. Christ is the Bread of heaven, and the flesh of Christ is the bread of heaven. There is an eating of Christ as the true Bread of heaven that happens in faith. And there is an eating of the flesh and a drinking of the blood of Christ that occurs

78

in the Sacrament of the Eucharist. Both of these truths belong together in such a way that one cannot reduce one of them to the other.

What is so striking in the statements about the sacramental eating is the realistic, even drastic, wording in John 6:51b–58: While Paul speaks of the *body* and blood of Christ, it is called *flesh* and blood in John. Where Paul speaks of fellowship in the body of Christ, fellowship in the blood of Christ, John is not afraid to speak of eating the body and drinking the blood, and he even uses for "eat," besides the ordinary word *esthiein*, the extremely harsh sounding *trōgein*, "chew." While Paul obviously consciously avoids the starkly realistic sounding expressions, John evidently delights in them. And it is just this drastic wording that has again and again prompted the suggestion that it must have a deeper, mystical meaning hidden behind it. Is it really correct to speak of the *flesh* of the Son of Man as the food of the Lord's Supper when Jesus Himself used the word *body?* Paul never would have put "flesh" in place of "body." Why was the evangelist not satisfied with the expressions that he found in Paul? That must be connected with John's interest in the word *sarx* in general. When he uses this word, either he speaks of the flesh in the sense of the transitory, sinful creature (1 John 2:16), the flesh that is at variance with the Spirit (John 3:6; 8:15) and that therefore is of no use (6:63), or he speaks of the flesh that the Logos has taken on (1:14; 1 John 4:2; 2 John 7). The statements about the flesh of the Son of Man belong naturally in this context. And now it becomes clear immediately why John does not take over the Pauline terminology but develops it in a more realistic direction. His principal antagonist is the Docetism of emerging Gnosticism (1 John 4:2), a spiritualistic Christianity that believes it is stating the highest thing possible of Jesus Christ when it regards Him as a divine being who had a heavenly body but no body of flesh. The representatives of this view would not have failed to exploit passages of the letters of Paul, for example, the statements that Christ was "in the likeness of men" and was "found in human form" (Phil. 2:7[–8]) or that flesh and blood cannot inherit the kingdom of God (1 Cor. 15:50). In the presence of the heresy of Docetism the terminology of Paul was no longer sufficient—just as later in the history of dogma newly appearing heresies again and again required the improvement of the terminology. (One thinks of the *homoousios* that had to serve as the defense against Arianism or of the development of Lutheran terminology about the Lord's Supper.) Therefore John had to define the Incarnation exactly as becoming flesh. And the same reason would have prompted the development of the terminology about the

Lord's Supper. If need be, one can understand the word *sōma* entirely spiritualistically, even though this is against Paul's meaning. Therefore, in order to accent the reality of the body unequivocally, John dares to say "flesh" instead of "body," something like the "resurrection of the dead" in the Eastern confessions of faith corresponds to the "resurrection of the flesh" in the Western Creed. In all these phrases "flesh" means nothing other than "true body." This theological use of the word *sarx* constitutes the protest against the spiritualization of redemption, against the dualistic world view that regards flesh in itself as evil, and so against the denial of the Incarnation. John 6:51b–58 is to be understood in this sense. The "flesh" of Christ here is nothing else than what the church later called "true body." Eating and drinking do not mean a physical eating in the usual sense. That would be the "Capernaitic" misunderstanding, which according to John 6:60ff. must have already very early caused people to become confused about the Christian faith, a misunderstanding that still pops up in the heathen reproach about the cannibalism that supposedly was practiced in the Christian divine service. Over against this misunderstanding the statement holds true: "It is the Spirit that gives life, the flesh is of no avail; the words that I have spoken to you are Spirit and life" (6:63). That does not mean that the flesh of Christ is of no use, as Luther already correctly saw. (Luther established the rule: "Whenever Spirit and flesh are set in contrast to each other in Scripture, there flesh cannot mean Christ's flesh but must mean the old Adam." [WA 26:375; cf. American Edition, 37:250].) Then the Incarnation would also be given up. But here flesh must refer to human flesh with its natural functions. The eating of the flesh, that is, of Christ's true body, is an eating, as far as what is eaten goes into our bodies, but it is not a *carnal* eating, not an eating that serves to build up our body. The effect of this eating is twofold: the entrance of Christ into the person ("He who eats My flesh and drinks My blood abides in Me, and I in him" [6:56].) and the possession of "life" (53), specifically, "eternal life" (54) now and in the resurrection. How this happens the Gospel does not tell us. It is simply a miracle, as much beyond human comprehension as any other of Christ's miracles and as the last things, with which this miracle goes together.

If one asks how John relates to Paul at this point, a real agreement is discovered here also. For Paul naturally did not teach a physical effect of the Lord's Supper only for the unworthy, even if in 1 Cor. 11:27ff. he only happens to speak about them. Both Paul and John would accept the expression with which the Antiochene Liturgy about the turn of the first century describes the gifts of the Eucharist (that Ignatius, *Ad Eph.*, 20. 2, did not formulate the expression himself but quoted it from the liturgy has been shown by Lietzmann, 257 [*Mass and Lord's Supper*, 210]):

pharmakon athanasias
antidotos tou mē apothanein
alla zēn en Iēsou Christō dia pantos.

Medicine of immortality,
Antidote that we die not
But live in Jesus always.

The Unity of the Lord's Supper in the New Testament

If Paul and John understood the Words of Institution literally—and the realization that this is the case has made more and more headway in the last generation—then only one way out remains for those who cannot credit Jesus with a realistic understanding. They must accept that the Lord's Supper has already undergone a development in the New Testament that has led to a different understanding of the Words of Institution, at variance with Jesus' original meaning. Now no one will deny that the Lord's Supper already experienced a history in the New Testament. Jesus' Last Supper, the breaking of bread in the first congregation, the Lord's Supper in the Pauline congregations, and the Sacrament of the flesh and blood of Christ that lies behind John 6:51b-58 are the stages of this history still recognizable today. In that history not only the external form but also the understanding of the Lord's Supper have unfolded. This development is further reflected in the expansion of the *verba testamenti* in the liturgical usage of the early church, which we have discussed, and especially in the addition of "for the forgiveness of sins" and of the command to go on doing it. While the former clearly represents only an elucidation of "for many," in regard to the command to repeat it must be asked whether it has not completely changed the original meaning of the Lord's Supper. If Jesus, as it is often supposed, gave no thought at all to a repetition of the celebration, then whoever first came up with the idea of repeating what had been a nonrecurring eschatological action would be the actual originator of the church's Sacrament of the Lord's Supper. In the same way, the transition from a symbolic to a literal understanding of the words of explanation would mean not just a development but a complete change of the original understanding of the Lord's Supper. Whoever subscribes to such a radical change must answer the question of when and for what reasons it would have happened. The transformation of a nonrecurring symbolic action into a Sacrament that can be repeated (and that means the creation of the Sacrament) could only be explained, if need be, out of the inner necessity of the early church, even if our sources give no reason for such an assumption. But this explanation breaks down completely over the question why one would have exchanged a figurative understanding of "This is My body" for a literal one. For one cannot consider Paul, John, and the church for which they speak to be so unthinking as not to realize the difficulties that the realistic interpretation brought with it. If "This is My body" must be understood literally, then that applies not only to the Lord's Supper celebrated in the church today but also more than ever to what Jesus observed with His disciples on the night before His death. It was not first a discovery of Zwingli, Calvin (*Inst.* 4. 17. 17), and modern exegesis that Jesus still stood before them physically as He gave the bread to His disciples with these words. The apostle who preserved for us the earliest report of what happened there certainly knew it also. He tells us what Jesus said, did, and ordained on that occasion.

Here lies the reason why the realistic statement of the Lord's Supper in Paul and John also cannot be derived from an influence of the Hellenistic mystery religions. That a parallel exists between the Lord's Supper and the sacrificial meals and communion celebrations of the mysteries Paul himself has noted. Even more than that, we may assume that the terminology of the apostle (e. g., the expression "the table of the Lord"; cf. H. Lietzmann, *Handbuch z. N. T.*, on 1 Cor. 10:21 and Preuschen-Bauer [Bauer-Arndt-Gingrich], *Wörterbuch*, under *trapeza*) and even his thoughts about the effects of the Lord's Supper have been influenced by his religious environment. As he, the great missionary to the Gentiles, understands Jesus as the Lord, the Kyrios, in contrasting Him with everything that bears the name "kyrios" in the Gentile world (1 Cor. 8:5f.), so he explains for himself and his congregations the koinonia with Christ that the Lord's Supper creates by contrasting it with the koinonia that is actually created between those who partake of the sacrificial meals and the demons who are there honored as lords [*Kyrioi*]. At one point, however, and that the most decisive point, this parallel is shattered. That a historical person at a historical time—"The Lord Jesus on the night when He was betrayed"—gave His disciples His body and His blood to eat and to drink is an assertion for which there is nothing comparable in the heathen cults. But on this assertion everything depends. For that action of Jesus was certainly for Paul not just the promise of something that would happen only after the Lord's resurrection and ascension, but it was the historical beginning, the institution, of the Lord's Supper. The fundamental difference that separates emerging Christianity from the mystery religions around it becomes clear precisely in the Lord's Supper. The heathen mystery cult rests on a myth. That Attis or Osiris died and rose again is myth, religious-poetic garb for a timeless truth, perhaps the truth valid always and everywhere that suffering leads to joy and death to life. It is nonsense to ask when the death of Osiris took place. This death is not a historical event, for the myth tells of things that lie beyond earthly history because they are timeless and eternal. It is quite the opposite with the death and resurrection of Jesus Christ. These did not happen in the timelessness of myth but at a specific time in earthly history: "Suffered *under Pontius Pilate . . . on the third day* He rose again from the dead."

The Lord's Supper is firmly anchored in this history according to the oldest witness we have of it in the New Testament. Its historical origin is *"on the night when He was betrayed."* (Because it depends on the *historical* and not the *calendar* date, the night is designated as the night of the betrayal, not as Passover night.) It would be a serious mistake to try to understand the account of the institution as "an etiological cult legend" (e. g., K. L. Schmidt, *RGG*² 1:9). It is as far removed from something like that as the historical message of the death and resurrection of Jesus is from one of the resurrection myths. The Lord's Supper stands and falls on the fact that it is the repetition of the Sacrament instituted by Jesus Himself. So Paul could not have understood it in any other way than that Jesus gave His disciples at the Last Supper the same thing that is received in the Lord's Supper of the church. But that the Redeemer, who is about to die as a true Man, gave His body and His blood to those who were His own to eat and to drink is utterly inconceivable to Hellenism and therefore an idea that could not have derived from Hellenistic influences.

Nothing shows more clearly how alien the Christian Lord's Supper was to ancient heathenism than the position that the ancient world took over against it. That through the consumption of holy food one took in the deity, its life and its powers, was a concept that heathen antiquity knew. Had the Lord's Supper been nothing else than a celebration of a communion in which consecrated food and consecrated drink bound the participants in the cult to one another and with their lord, it would have been inconceivable that the ancient world would have taken such strong offense at it. The reproach of "Thyestian meals," that is, cultic cannibalism, that accompanied the ancient church through the whole period of persecution can only be explained if the Lord's Supper was something that ancient heathenism was absolutely incapable of understanding. That calumny cannot be explained as though occasionally the suspicion of ritual murder was expressed, similar to that aroused by other secret cults. Since it recurs continually, it must have its root in a possible misunderstanding of the Lord's Supper. (In the same way the reproach of indecency attached to the "holy kiss" [e. g., Rom. 16:16; 1 Cor. 16:20; 1 Peter 5:14], with which the Lord's Supper began, is explained.) But if the thought that at the Christian altar one partook of the body and blood of Christ, that the flesh of the Son of Man was eaten, and His blood was drunk, aroused such strong offense, then one cannot derive such thinking from the influence of the mysteries.

But the transition to sacramental realism also cannot be explained as a result of a development purely within the church. Neither Paul nor the church from which Paul took over the liturgical account of the institution could have replaced an older symbolic-spiritualistic understanding of the Lord's Supper with a realistic one. If Paul, as Lietzmann thinks, really were the originator of a second type of Lord's Supper, then it would be inconceivable that among the charges raised by his opponents against him one never finds one that he falsified the Lord's Supper. Of the church before Paul, however, we may only assert that it changed the original meaning of the Lord's Supper if clues could be found that there ever was a Lord's Supper that was not a commemoration of the death of Christ, not a repetition of the Lord's Supper that was instituted by Him, and in which the Words of Institution either were missing or were understood in some other way than literally. There are no such clues. Neither the breaking of bread in Acts nor the Lord's Supper in the *Didache* can be cited in support of that. If the celebration took place "with gladness" according to Acts 2:47, then it can surely be assumed that this was also the case when Paul presided over the breaking of bread as Acts 20:7–11 reports. When did the Lord's Supper ever lack the character of the Eucharist? Since when should remembering the Lord's death and joyful thanksgiving for His redemption be regarded as mutually exclusive? And if reference to Jesus' death and mention of the Words of Institution are missing from the prayers of the Lord's Supper in the *Didache*, it should not be forgotten that we do not have the complete liturgy of the church that stands behind the *Didache*. How little the argument from silence is valid in this area is shown by Paul himself. If the circumstances in Corinth had not made it necessary for him on this one occasion to speak of the Lord's Supper, then surely modern New Testament scholarship would have asserted that the Lord's Supper was not celebrated at all in his congregations. For in his other letters he does not say a word about it.

So we can come to no other conclusion than that the Lord's Supper, from Jesus' Last Supper to the Sacrament of the church, is a unity, as the Fourth Gospel testifies. Its names vary; the rite has changed; the understanding of the celebration deepened little by little. But it is one and the same Lord's Supper that sees its history in this development. What remains the same in all stages of this development are the Words of Institution. And that can not only be the wording, which preserves itself in the main except for minor variations, but must also clearly be its meaning. In the church of the New Testament it was never understood in any other way than in the sense that Jesus Christ Himself gave His disciples His true body and His true blood to eat and to drink at the Last Supper and that in the Lord's Supper of the church He still does the same. Since it can absolutely not be seen why the apostles should have introduced this interpretation of the Lord's Supper into the church, and since, as we have pointed out, the Words of Institution cannot be understood as a parable or in some other figurative sense, no other possibility remains at all than to accept that Jesus Himself intended for the Lord's Supper to be understood in this way.

Jesus Himself said and meant that the bread is His body, the wine in the cup is His covenant blood. It is a different question whether one believes Him when He says this or not, whether one regards this statement as significant or not. The experiences of New Testament scholarship of the last generation should be a warning for us against the error of answering the question about the historical authenticity of Jesus' sayings on the basis of whether one agrees with them or not. How many sayings [*Logia*], how many statements of the New Testament witnesses have been denied Jesus because someone regarded it as impossible that they came from His lips! It has been denied that He regarded Himself as the Messiah, that He spoke of the saving significance of His death. Today we know that His whole activity, suffering, and death can only be understood under the assumption that He knew Himself to be the Messiah-Son of Man and that He applied to Himself and fulfilled the prophecy of the Suffering Servant of God (see Otto Procksch, "Passa und Abendmahl," *Vom Sakrament des Altars*, ed. Hermann Sasse [1941], 25). If one looks at what historical-critical theology of the last century has at one time or another declared authentic or inauthentic in the gospels, one is almost tempted to find there the rule: Theological statements that this theology no longer understood or did not regard as correct were denied to Jesus. They were laid at the door of anonymous tradition of the congregation or of the apostles, Paul most of all, but Jesus was not credited with them. Thus Heitmüller (*Taufe und Abendmahl*, 56) says of Luther's understanding of "This is My body":

> That this understanding is very old, that it, or at least something like it, is already to be found in early Christianity, even in Paul, and that the writers and the first readers of the gospels understood the words in such a way is certain. . . . All of this, however, does not justify the view that Jesus Himself meant these words in this way. No less than everything speaks against this view.

On closer examination, this "everything" consists of three arguments: The copula "is" was probably not spoken in Aramaic; furthermore, "is" can be used for "signifies"; and third, Jesus still stood physically in front of His disciples when He spoke the words of the Last Supper. As if Paul, the apostles, and the early church had no notion of that "everything"! If Heitmüller can credit the authors of the gospels with understanding the *verba testamenti* literally after all, why can he not credit Jesus with that? Is it out of respect for the Lord, to whom he would not want to ascribe an obviously absurd statement? Or does he need Jesus' authority to authenticate his own view? In any case, the historian must be on his guard against measuring Jesus and the apostles by two different standards and declaring the ideas with which he himself does not agree to be a garnishing by the apostles. Because some have not guarded against this danger, the distance between Jesus and the early church and between Jesus and Paul could be exaggerated in recent scholarship in a way that does violence to the historical reality. As far as the Words of Institution are concerned, however, there is no serious historical basis for the assumption that Jesus meant something essentially different by them than the early church and the writers of the gospels. Least of all is that a sufficient reason for the historian as such not to understand the meaning of the Words of Institution.

The Theological Meaning of the Lord's Supper

Our historical inquiry into the origin of the Christian Lord's Supper ended with the discovery of what Jesus said and did at the first celebration of the Lord's Supper and with the well-founded supposition that the Words of Institution already at that time said nothing else than that with the bread and the cup He gave those who took part in the celebration His true body and His true blood to eat and to drink. Historical research is not able to get to the bottom of the meaning of this assertion, which at first sounds absurd. But this is not to say that it has no meaning. The disciples of Jesus obviously did not feel it was senseless. They did not, as on other occasions, say: "Explain to us the parable" (Matt. 13:36; 15:15), for they apparently knew that it was not a matter of a parable here. They also did not express the disgruntled astonishment with which the natural man has always reacted to the words of the Lord's Supper and that is characteristically expressed in John 6:60: "This is a hard saying; who can listen to it?" Certainly their understanding would only have been a very weak one, and who could expect more from them? They accepted the Lord's Supper just as they accepted Jesus' prophecy of His suffering, death, and resurrection after an initial protest. What applies to the announcements of the Passion must certainly also be accepted of the words about the Lord's Supper: the full understanding of it dawns on the disciples only after Easter. Yet already at the Last Supper they must have understood enough that this action and the words that accompanied it had a deep meaning. Under the assumption that this was Jesus, as He had let Himself be known by them, they clearly received what He said about His body and blood, words that would have been an absurdity coming from any other mouth, as absolutely meaningful. Under this assumption and *only* under this assumption was there at that time and is there now an understanding of the Lord's Supper.

Therefore, only in theological statements can what the Lord's Supper is be expressed, for theological statements in the strict sense of Christian theology are statements based on the assumption that Jesus Christ is the Son of God, who became man, true God, begotten of the Father from eternity, and also true Man, born of the Virgin Mary; that He died on the cross as the Lamb of God, who bears the sin of the world; that He rose bodily from the dead; that He is exalted at the Father's right hand; and that He will return in glory to judge the living and the dead. Because the Lord's Supper can only be understood on this assumption, it is totally incomprehensible to the world, which does not believe in Christ, and the church at all times has gotten into the greatest difficulty when it was asked by the world, and that includes historical and religious scholarship, what the Lord's Supper really is. One can just as little make it clear to a person who does not believe in Jesus Christ as one can explain to him the essence and effect of Baptism. This explains the silence with which the early church already surrounded the Lord's Supper and that was only broken when it became a question of confronting the worst calumnies. These calumnies themselves, just like the assertions of strangeness and the lack of comprehension in later times, are a confirmation that the Lord's Supper has always been a riddle to the world, the Words of Institution always an absurdity.

There, however, where one shares that faith, the Lord's Supper has always been regarded as one of the deepest mysteries of the Christian faith and the most holy part of the Christian divine service. What it meant for the church of the New Testament becomes clear if one tries to imagine the original church in Jerusalem without the breaking of bread or the Pauline congregations without the Lord's Supper. It is impossible. A Lord's Day without the Lord's Supper is absolutely unthinkable in the New Testament. Without the Eucharist the church would have ceased to be church. It would no longer exist at all. And that goes for the whole New Testament, also for those writings in which the Lord's Supper is not directly mentioned; even there it stands in the background as a fact that belongs to the essence of the church. All this is only clearly understood, however, if all that Jesus Christ is and all that He brought, His whole person and His whole work, is indissolubly connected with the Lord's Supper. That is in fact the case, and no one else than Jesus Himself has made the connection.

Therein lies the meaning of the action that we call the institution of the Lord's Supper. It is the last act of Jesus before His death, an act of unfathomable profoundness and immeasurable consequences. In the face of death, which is both the end and the fulfillment of His life's work on earth, *Jesus gives His disciples redemption*. What until then was only the object of the promise comes true in the moment when the Lord gives them His body and His blood. Without the institution of the Lord's Supper the Gospel could be misunderstood as a teaching about redemption and Jesus Himself as the greatest of the prophets of the coming Kingdom. This misunderstanding is now no longer possible. With the Words of Institution the prophetic office of Christ is fulfilled, and His high priestly work begins. From now on wherever this Sacrament is repeated, wherever the Words of Institution resound anew, there redemption is something more than the object of the promise. It is actually given to whoever receives the Sacrament in faith. Under the forms of bread and wine what Christ sacrificed as "High Priest forever" (Heb. 6:20) and as "the Lamb of God, who takes away the sin of the world"

(John 1:29) in the *one* sacrifice of the cross "for many" is received. It is actually received just as the flesh of the Passover lamb is received by all who celebrate the Passover. So the Lord's Supper is a sacrificial meal, and one could even say with the Council of Trent that it is *memoria, repraesentatio,* and *applicatio* of Christ's sacrifice if the further formulations of Trent and of other Roman doctrinal statements did not give the words *repraesentatio* and *applicatio* yet another meaning that is not compatible with the New Testament. But that the Lord's Supper is the re-presentation of Christ's sacrifice and the real bestowal of what is gained through this sacrifice is the clear teaching of the New Testament. If one wants to understand it as a sacrificial meal only figuratively, then the sacrifice of Christ on the cross would also have to be understood figuratively. The Lord's Supper confirms the sacrificial meaning of the death of Christ by again and again reminding Christendom that it is redeemed by an actual sacrifice in the sense of the words: "Without the shedding of blood there is no forgiveness of sins" (Heb. 9:22). Understood as a sacrificial meal, it forms a bulwark against the view, widespread also in modern Christendom, that the death of Christ is to be thought of only figuratively as a sacrifice, something like the heroic death of a soldier for his country or the sacrifice of a mother for her child.

That Jesus Himself understood the Last Supper as a sacrificial meal in this sense is shown by the clear connections between the action and the words of Jesus on the one hand and the Passover celebration and sacrificial thought in the Old Testament on the other. They have been expertly set forth in the first chapter of this book [Procksch, "Passa und Abendmahl," *Vom Sakrament des Altars,* 11–25]. These connections could not have been introduced only later into the Lord's Supper tradition. This is proved by the great difficulty that the idea of the blood of Christ causes in this connection. That the body of Christ is eaten, in fact *must* be eaten, as the body of the true Passover lamb is understandable if the parallel between the Passover and the Lord's Supper is really to be valid. But the idea of partaking of blood had to cause most serious offense for those whose thinking was schooled in the Old Testament. For partaking of blood was strictly forbidden in the Old Testament, and even the parallel between the covenant blood in Exodus 24:8 and the covenant blood in the Words of Institution is seriously distorted when the latter is given to the disciples to drink. The difficulty is so great that one could credit no one, least of all Paul or John, with having burdened the idea of the Lord's Supper with it after the event.

There is really no other possibility than the assumption that Jesus Himself is the originator of the idea that not only is His body taken as that of the "Lamb without blemish or spot" (1 Pet. 1:19) but also His blood. Parenthetically we may note that no doctrine of the Lord's Supper, not even the Zwinglian, can get over this difficulty, because even the representatives of the symbolic interpretation must grant that Jesus must have been speaking at least parabolically about the drinking of His blood. But if Jesus did express this idea that was so offensive to Jewish and perhaps to all human thought, then His meaning could only have been the following: Partaking of blood is forbidden in the old covenant because according to Lev. 17:11 the body's life is in the blood and because the life belongs to God. But the life of Jesus has been offered up for men. It should be for their benefit. For here men do not bring a sacrifice to God through a priest, but the High Priest offers Himself as a sacrifice to God for the sake of men. That Christ gives His blood to those redeemed by Him to drink is the strongest expression of the fact that He sacrifices Himself for men entirely, unreservedly, and completely. He gives His whole life for men without any kind of reservation. That is the sacrifice of perfect love. And wherever the Lord's Supper is celebrated, the blessing of this sacrifice is given to men. Therefore the cup in the Lord's Supper is particularly the most significant expression of the "for many," "given and shed for you for the forgiveness of sins."

Since the Lord's Supper is such an actualization, *an actual appropriation of redemption*—and not merely a promise and proclamation of it—it is *the fulfillment of salvation history*. As the redeeming work of Christ finds its fulfillment in it, so also does the great history of redemption, at whose end stands the cross of the Lord. That explains why a series of Old Testament types and prophecies points to the Lord's Supper and why it cannot be understood merely as the fulfillment of an individual one of these (see on this point Simon Schöffel, *Offenbarung Gottes in Abendmahl* [1938], 33ff.). As surely as the Lord's Supper is first of all to be understood from the *Passover*, as the act of its institution shows, so it is certainly also to be understood as the true *bread from heaven*, the manna of the end time, as is taught already in 1 Cor. 10:1ff. and John 6. Both Jeremiah's promise of the new *covenant* (31:31ff.) and what Isaiah 53 says about the *death of the Servant of God for "many"* are fulfilled in it. In the Lord's Supper the one who acts is at the same time the fulfiller and the fulfillment of all prophecies of the Old Testament about the coming redemption. Hence the Lord's Supper is the *memorial meal* of the accomplished redemption. As in the Passover one commemorated the redeeming act of God, who wondrously delivered His people from the slavery of Egypt, so the Lord's Supper should be observed "in remembrance of Me." And one can probably say that never has a command found a truer and more comprehensive fulfillment than the instruction: "This do in remembrance of Me," regardless of whether this instruction was pronounced by Jesus or whether it was included in the institution by implication. The historical character of the Christian faith, which always appeals to historical facts because it lives by the redemption that happened at a particular time in history, is nowhere more clearly discernible than in the fact that the celebration that stands at the center of the divine service is a celebration "in remembrance of Me." Where has a historical event been more faithfully remembered than is the death of Christ in the Lord's Supper of His church? There is no other event in the history of antiquity that is so imprinted in the memory of people and lives on throughout the world today. The Lord's Supper has kept this memory so deeply alive precisely because it is even more than a memorial meal. It is not only a celebration of reminiscence like the Passover, in which the human spirit recalled the past for itself, but it is a genuine, actual *bringing into the present* of God's redeeming act through the gift of the body and blood of Christ.

Like the past, the *future* also becomes present in the Lord's Supper. It is part of the essence of the Lord's Supper that it is a wonderful *anticipation of the future.* As the Last Supper was perhaps the anticipation of the Passover, which should not have been celebrated until the next day (see on this, besides Procksch, "Passa und Abendmahl," 23, also Th. Kliefoth, *Liturgische Abhandlungen* [1858], 4:186f.), so was the first Lord's Supper in any case already the sacrificial meal in which in a miraculous way—the institution of the Lord's Supper does not belong to the parables but to the miracles of Jesus—the participants actually received what was to be offered the following day on the cross. (It is never the task of theology to explain miracles [least of all to explain them away], but to state them and to expound their meaning in the light of the whole of divine revelation. In this sense the church has always pointed to the miracle of the Transfiguration in Matt. 17:2 as an analogy of the miracle of the Lord's Supper. What the anticipation involves reminds us of the words of Kliefoth [p. 187]: "One may not infer the weakness of the Lord's Supper held on the night of the betrayal from this anticipation, for as good as the blood of Christ was, before it was shed, to make the blood of goats and calves valid, so it also is with the wine in this anticipated Lord's Supper.")

The research of the last generation has legitimately emphasized that in the whole New Testament the Lord's Supper is the anticipation on earth of the Messianic banquet. Wherever it is celebrated, all eyes are turned toward the end. The Word of Jesus that He would not drink again of the fruit of the vine "until that day when I drink it new in the kingdom of God" (Mark 14:25) is matched by Paul's comment that in the Lord's Supper the congregation proclaims the Lord's death "until He comes" (1 Cor. 11:26). John also looks from the Lord's Supper to the resurrection of the dead "at the last day" (6:54), and it is certainly no accident that the few fragments of the earliest liturgies of the Lord's Supper that have been preserved for us are alive with a glowing hope of the Parousia. This is found in Paul (1 Cor. 16:22) and in the *Didache* (10. 6) preserved in the Aramaic *Maranatha*, which is translated at the end of the New Testament as "Come, Lord Jesus" (Rev. 22:20; that this prayer belongs to the liturgy of the Lord's Supper Lietzmann, *Messe und Abendmahl*, 237, demonstrates convincingly), and in the Eucharistic prayers of the *Didache*.

The eschatological character of the Lord's Supper may not, of course, be understood as if this Sacrament is *only* understood on the basis of Christian hope as a celebration in which the church brings its eschatological expectations impressively into its consciousness. Much rather the hope of the Lord's return and the coming Kingdom is so powerfully alive in this celebration because the Lord's Supper, as the celebration of Christ's real presence, already includes a fulfillment of that expectation. Whoever partakes of it already now sits at the table of the Lord, whose guest he will be one day in the kingdom of God. The same Lord, whose coming in glory one implores in the Eucharistic prayers, is already present in the celebration of the Eucharist. Thus the prayer "Come, Lord Jesus" retains its eschatological meaning, but at the same time it carries the meaning expressed in an early liturgical prayer (in the Mozarabic liturgy, quoted according to Lietzmann, *Messe und Abendmahl*, 105 [*Mass and Lord's Supper*, 86]): "Be present, be present, Jesus, good priest, among us, as also you will be in the midst of your disciples." Because Jesus Christ is really present as High Priest and sacrificial Lamb in this celebration, the custom, taken over from the synagogue service, of singing the Sanctus, the song of the seraphim in the presence of God, at the celebration of the Eucharist has taken on an especially profound meaning. The celebration of the Lord's Supper as the church's divine service has become the counterpart of the divine service that takes place in heaven, an idea that is expressed in Rev. 4

(cf. also 1 Clement 34:6 where, in addition to Is. 6:3, Dan. 7:10 is quoted: "Ten thousand times ten thousand stood before Him, and a thousand thousands served Him"). Thus in the Lord's Supper the boundaries of space and time are overcome: Heaven and earth become one, the incalculable interval that separates the present moment of the church from the future kingdom of God is bridged.

From this it becomes easy to understand what the Lord's Supper must mean for the church's *preservation*, as it turned out that the eschatological expectations, as the apostolic age cherished them, did not come to fulfillment. Humanly speaking, there was perhaps never a deeper disappointment than the nonappearance of the Parousia, which they had believed to be so near. How was it possible for the church to survive this disappointment? How was it able to preserve hope for the Day of Jesus Christ through so many centuries in spite of the mockery of the world and doubt in its own ranks? The Lord's Supper alone has made that possible. It is the Sacrament of the church that waits for the fulfillment of the promises. The church that celebrates it understands itself to be the new people of God, who have been freed from the slavery of Egypt but have not yet arrived in the Promised Land. It is what later came to be called food of travelers [*cibus viatorum*], eaten in haste by pilgrims like the first Passover according to Ex. 12:11: "In this manner you shall eat it: your loins girded, your sandals on your feet, and your staff in your hand; and you shall eat it in haste. It is the Lord's passover." It is food for travelers like the manna, with which Paul and John already compared it. Like Israel in the wilderness was miraculously saved by the "spiritual food" (1 Cor. 10:1ff.) manna, by the "bread from heaven" (John 6:32, 50f., 58; cf. Psalm 78:24), from death by starvation, so the church is preserved on its journey through the wilderness of this world by the miracle of the Lord's Supper. The situation of the church with the Lord's Supper is pictured in no better way than in these Old Testament types. With the traveling staff in hand, in the wilderness between Egypt and the Promised Land, as those who have been freed from the slavery of the old age but have not yet arrived in the land of freedom, in the twilight between the ages Christians eat their Lord's Passover, they live on the bread of heaven, when they celebrate the Lord's Supper. And no one can understand this Sacrament who does not understand this situation, that is, who does not himself belong to these travelers.

Finally, there is yet one more sense in which the Lord's Supper is an actualization of the redemption achieved by Christ. F. Kattenbusch

("Der Quellort der Kirchenidee" in *Festgabe für A. v. Harnack* [1921], 168f.) once raised the questions, whether, when, and how Jesus actually fulfills His promise in Matt. 16:18 that He would build His church, and he answered in this way: "The Lord's Supper was the act by which He founded His church (*ekklēsia*), His congregation." Even if we must stick to the fact that the church first entered into history on the basis of the events of Easter and Pentecost—the significance of Peter also first became clear at that time—Kattenbusch's thesis nevertheless doubtlessly contains a correct perception. For if the Twelve represent the 12 tribes of Israel and their circle is therefore the representation of the people of God who believe in Jesus as the Messiah, then they are already the church insofar as there can be a church before the death and resurrection of Jesus. Then the Last Supper, which Jesus celebrated with them as the Passover of the new covenant, is really the *organization of the new people of God*. At the same time He establishes the relationship that will exist from then on between Him and His church—"My church" [*mou tēn ekklēsian*] He emphasizes in Matt. 16:18.

The fellowship binding Him with the church that celebrates the Lord's Supper is more than a table fellowship. His presence there is more than the presence for which the prayer quoted above asked: "Be present . . . among us, as you will be in the midst of your disciples." Because He is not only the host but also the Passover lamb, therefore "what counts most is not His table fellowship with the disciples but His incorporation into the disciples under the bread and wine, as the Passover lamb was incorporated into the celebrating congregation" (Procksch, 24). Clearly, this fellowship, this koinonia, that binds Christ to His church and the members of the church to one another is something utterly unique, a koinonia for which there is no analogy at all either in the religious fellowships of the world or in human community life. Paul expresses the unparalleled nature of this fellowship when he calls the church the *body of Christ*. What does he mean by that? No explanation is needed if a form of community is called a corpus, a body in the sense of a corporation. If we find that Paul is merely applying to the church the simile common in ancient sociology of a body and its members, there is no problem at all; and it would be immediately understood if the apostle said of the church in this sense: "We, though many, are one body in Christ" (Rom. 12:5). The puzzle begins at the point where Paul no longer designates the church as a body in Christ but as the body of Christ (1 Cor. 12:27; cf. v. 13; Col. 1:18; Eph. 1:23; 4:12, 16). For the statement "You are the body of Christ" (1 Cor. 12:27) contains much more than a comparison between the church and a body. The idea that the church is the body of Christ in Paul is indissolubly bound up with his view of the Lord's Supper, as 1 Cor. 10:17 shows: "Because there is *one* bread, we who are many are *one* body, for we all partake of the *one* bread." The koinonia of the body of Christ that the Lord's Supper effects is, as we have shown earlier, the actual partaking of, the closest fellowship with, the body of Christ, which is given to us with the bread. It is at the same time, as we now recognize, membership in the church as the body of Christ. (Even if Ephesians and even—though there is no serious basis for it—Colossians would have to be regarded as deutero-Pauline, the usage "body of Christ" for the church would still be secured for Paul through 1 Cor. 12:27. It is a fabrication for H. Schlier, *Christus und die Kirche im Epheserbrief* [1930], 41, to understand "body of Christ" in 1 Cor. 12:27 as "a body that belongs to Christ" and to assert: "It should not be said as in Ephesians that they [i. e., the Christians] are the body of Christ and His members [the *autou* with *melē* is missing in Paul!]." In 1 Cor. 6:15 the bodies of Christians are explicitly called members of Christ. The progress in Col. and Eph. in the doctrine of the body of Christ lies only in the introduction of the idea of Christ as the Head of the church.)

There is then in Paul a double usage of the expression "body of Christ." Body of Christ is the bread of the Lord's Supper, but body of Christ is also the church. Both statements are to be understood quite realistically in the meaning of the apostle. Because the bread of the Lord's Supper is the body of Christ, therefore the church is the body of Christ. How are we to understand this? The *corpus Christi* that is in, with, and under the church is to the *corpus Christi* that is in, with, and under the bread of the Lord's Supper apparently as the church itself is to the bread of the Lord's Supper. As this *one* bread binds Christians to the unity of the church, so the true body of the Lord, which is received in the Lord's Supper, makes the church to be the body of Christ. We must recall that according to the view of the apostolic age the church above all comes into view in the celebration of the Lord's Supper. When the heavenly food of the body of Christ goes into us, we at the same time go into this body. When Christ embodies Himself in us, we are at the same time embodied in Him. This corresponds exactly with what is said in John 6:56 about this double communion: "He who eats My flesh and drinks My blood abides in Me, and I in him." When the heavenly body of Christ is given to us Christians in the Lord's Supper, we become the church as the body of Christ on earth. According to the New Testament, then, there is not only the body of Christ that, exalted at the right hand of the Father, is truly given to us as heavenly food in the Sacrament of the Altar, but there is also, as a result and effect of this heavenly gift, what theology later called the *corpus Christi mysticum* (the expression has been adopted also by Lutheran theology, e. g., by John Gerhard, who speaks of *corpus Christi personale* and *corpus Christi mysticum* [*Loci* 22. 3—Preuss ed., 5:263ff.]), the church, which not only *resembles* a body but *is* the body of Christ on earth. Both belong inseparably together, just as the Lord's Supper and the church go together and, rightly understood, are one. Where the Lord's true body is received in the Sacrament, it does not remain without effect in the world. There the church is built as the body of Christ on earth and grows toward the consummation (Eph. 4:12–16).

Therefore, the Lord's Supper as "Holy Communion," as one may call it in this respect (see on this Paul Althaus, *Communio sanctorum* [1929], 75ff.), creates the fellowship of the church, the deepest fellowship with God and with all the children of God that there can be for us human beings. It is a fellowship that God has established in His gracious condescension to us sinners through the incarnation of His Son and that is renewed in every celebration of the Lord's Supper. He, the *Deus incarnatus*, who for our sake took flesh and blood, stoops down to us so low that He not only lives among us but in us, and we can do nothing else than speak the words of the centurion with the old liturgies of the Lord's Supper: "Lord, I am not worthy to have you come under my roof."

This fellowship is not only spiritual, as Christian idealism has always thought, but spiritual-physical [*geistleiblich*], just as the redeeming work of Christ affects the whole person, body and soul. One can only understand the Lord's Supper of the New Testament and its meaning for the church if one does not forget what the modern Christian unfortunately has forgotten again and again, that we belong to the church not only according to the spirit but also according to the body: "Do you not know that your bodies are members of Christ?" (1 Cor. 6:15). Therefore, as the New Testament makes quite clear, the Lord's Supper stands as the future becoming present in connection with the resurrection of the body. The Bible does not tell us the how of this connection. But the fact of this connection is clearly certified for us, as we saw in the discussion of John 6: "He who eats My flesh and drinks My blood has eternal life, and I will raise him up at the last day" (v. 54). Not only our souls but also our bodies belong to the Incarnate One, who has redeemed us body and soul. So the church according to its deepest essence is the body of Christ, and the Originator of the Lord's Supper also became the Founder of the church when He gave His disciples the bread with the words pregnant with meaning: "This is My body."

THE LORD'S SUPPER IN THE LUTHERAN CHURCH

Letter to Lutheran Pastors, No. 6
May 1949

Dear Brothers in the Ministry!

1.

We are unjustly accused of having abolished the Mass. Without boasting, it is manifest that the Mass is observed among us with greater devotion and more earnestness than among our opponents. Moreover, the people are instructed often and with great diligence concerning the holy sacrament, why it was instituted, and how it is to be used (namely, as a comfort for terrified consciences) in order that the people may be drawn to the Communion and Mass. The people are also given instruction about other false teachings concerning the sacrament. Meanwhile no conspicuous changes have been made in the public ceremonies of the Mass. [AC 24 1-2]

It is good for us Lutherans of today to remember that our fathers once could have said such a thing in Article 24 of the Augsburg Confession. It makes us aware of the quite enormous difference between our divine service and that of the Reformation and how far removed our modern understanding of the Lord's Supper is.

Who of us today would still dare to state that we have not abolished the Mass, the divine service comprising the proclamation of the Word and the Lord's Supper? No Christian of the Reformation, apart from the followers of the Reformation at Zurich and Geneva, could conceive of a Sunday divine service without the Lord's Supper, just as already in the church of the New Testament there was no Lord's Day without the Lord's Supper. And no one probably would dare to maintain that this divine service was celebrated with greater devotion and earnestness than by the Catholics.

If one asks for the secret of the vitality of the Catholic Church even in our time, one would have to admit that it is not its hierarchical organization, not its cult of saints and relics, not even, as many suppose, its traditional political astuteness that gives it its inner strength and predominance, but the fact that it celebrates the Sacrament of the Altar uninterruptedly throughout the world. This determines its whole life, even its whole theology.

To be sure, this Lord's Supper has been mutilated by the withdrawal of the cup from the laity. Certainly, false ideas about man's cooperation in salvation have gotten in since the intrusion of the early Christian notions of sacrifice that were, however, alien to the New Testament. It would be amazing indeed if what we must call the great errors of Catholicism had not gained a hold right here in this Holy of Holies of the church. The veneration of the consecrated host outside the celebration of the Sacrament, which was alien to the early church and still is to the Eastern Church but which first belonged to the later Middle Ages, is one of these errors, and it primarily produced the reaction of the Reformed false doctrine. Even Catholic theologians, who stand firmly on the dogmatic foundation of their church, readily admit that the Christian place of worship is not the house of God primarily or essentially because of the presence in it of the Eucharistic Christ in the tabernacle.

Traditional Protestantism criticizes much too easily when it places these things in the foreground, which for Catholics, at least for Catholic priests and laymen schooled in the modern liturgical movement, are not really what is essential, just as it is also a dangerous prejudice on the evangelical side to suppose that the external pomp, splendor, and beauty of the Catholic divine service constitutes its essence, as if it could not also be celebrated in puritan simplicity and meagerness. What the church of the Lutheran Reformation possessed and what modern Protestantism has lost, what Catholicism before the Reformation had largely forgotten and what modern Catholicism has largely learned to understand again is the simple truth of faith in the real presence of the true body and blood of our Lord Jesus Christ in, with, and under the forms of bread and wine in Holy Communion.

Concerning that truth the congregations of the Lutheran Reformation were "instructed often and with the greatest diligence," both adults and children. The Sixth Chief Part of the Catechism was written just for the instruction of children. If one hears again and again nowadays that children cannot understand it or not yet understand it, if modern Protestant catechetical instruction has almost become the art of distilling out of these plain words written for fathers of the house and their children a doctrine that swings somewhere between Zwingli and Calvin and is presented as Lutheranism simply because it is not blatant Zwinglianism, then one certainly is no longer surprised if the instruction that Article 24 of the Augsburg Confession has in mind scarcely happens any more. Then it is even less surprising that "instruction against other false teaching concerning the Sacrament" no longer takes place and that it is regarded as nothing but tactlessness or a violation of Christian love.

However, we may also then not be surprised if people no longer know "why the Sacrament was instituted and how it is to be used," that troubled consciences are not comforted by it, and theologians hunt in vain for a means "by which people are drawn to Communion and Mass." As appealing as the efforts of modern liturgical movements such as the Berneuchener and those like them to renew Holy Communion and the evangelical divine service may be, all these movements remain a liturgical handicraft for an aesthetic-religious elite that finds refuge from the real needs of our time in the incense cloud of a religious world where one dreams of sacrifice and transformation, of the bringing into the present of the sacrifice of Golgotha, where one fears nothing except Luther's plain confession of the real presence of the true body and blood of Christ in, with, and under the elements of bread and wine. But this proves that sacrifice, re-presentation, and transformation are only words that have next to nothing to do with Catholic *doctrine*, are not dangerous to it, but at the most lead people who are tired of this rhetoric to Rome.

The teaching that goes on is neither Lutheran nor Catholic; it is not even Reformed, though it is closest to the Reformed doctrine. One really does not teach at all; one only discusses and meditates (but not in the sense of the meditation of the great Christians of the past) and has nonbinding conversations, whose results, nevertheless, are to be binding for whole churches. But the people's hunger for the bread of life remains unsatisfied. The yearning for Christ, who according to His true divinity and humanity is present with His church in His means of grace for all time to the world's end, remains unappeased. For our theologians do not know whether that is the case, and if they do know it, they talk as if they were not quite sure. The Christian congregations and the people who are today looking longingly to the church want to know. They do not want to know whether the Catechism speaks "too directly," "too unguardedly," or "not dialectically enough," but whether what it says is true.

2.

Because they knew what they received there, the people of the old Lutheran Church went to Holy Communion. Because they know that at the altar they receive the body of Christ, Catholics in our time are going to Communion in ever growing number. Because they no longer know for sure what is received in the Sacrament of the Altar, Protestants, even those who call themselves Lutheran, are going to the Lord's Table in ever smaller numbers, and all efforts to make the congregations appreciate the German Mass of the Lutheran Reformation again have so far failed, and this is not due merely to technical difficulties. The only exception where there is a growing participation in the Lord's Supper by Protestants is the custom of concluding church rallies with a common celebration of the Lord's Supper. To what extent that is actually progress in the use of the Sacrament of the Altar will be discussed later.

General church statistics of ecclesiastical Germany inform us that out of 100 communions, more than 99 are by Catholics and less than one is by Protestants. However one may explain this number theologically, it is a simple fact that the Sacrament of the Altar plays an almost vanishing role in the life of evangelical Christendom, while it has become more or less a distinctive mark of Catholicism and its divine service. The reason for this can only be that the modern Protestant, also the modern theologian, indeed even the Lutheran pastor of our day, has become uncertain in his belief about the Sacrament and accordingly in his teaching about the Sacrament and therefore unable to "instruct" the congregation "often and with great diligence concerning the Lord's Supper," as our Confession takes it for granted as self-evident.

What is the reason for this? Why could the pastors of the 16th century do it, and why can we do it no more, despite the advances in the investigation of the New Testament and of the history of the Sacrament from both the dogmatic and the liturgical sides? The error must lie in our theology, to which Goethe's profound word applies: "We have studied ourselves out of life."

All genuine theology must proceed from the principle of speaking where God's Word speaks and being silent when God's Word is silent. For this reason Luther is the greatest teacher of the church for us, because he held unshaken to this principle even when the great temptation came to him, in which even the greatest theologians have always been caught at some point, to let something else hold sway in addition to the Word of God. The most difficult temptation for him, the basically conservative theologian, was traditionalism. He had held on to the traditional liturgy of the Mass with tenacious allegiance (even the Latin language at first). He had preserved the ancient liturgical forms and thereby saved them for the Lutheran Church. But with the sure sense of feeling of a theologian rooted in Scripture, he had recognized where already in the first century before the canon was completed something foreign from Judaism and paganism broke into the church, something that no apostle had taught: the sacrifice that man offers in the Lord's Supper. All traditionalistic theologians of our time, even those who regard themselves as good Lutherans, try to revive the sacrifice of the Mass in some way. In this matter Luther was unrelenting. With the theological penetration that was uniquely his he perceived that any concession at this point would mean a surrender both of *sola scriptura* and of *sola gratia*, which belong inseparably together.

The Lutheran Church knew with the Reformer that the word "sacrifice" is also used in Scripture in the figurative sense. If every prayer of praise and thanksgiving can be called a sacrifice, why not also the *Eucharistia*, the great prayer that was spoken at the Lord's Supper, and along with it the Lord's Supper itself? Chemnitz and other theologians put this question to themselves very earnestly. Their answer was that we are not here dealing with an adiaphoron any longer because the Roman Church here understands the word "sacrifice" in the strict sense of an atoning sacrifice, and one must repel this misconception. With the same seriousness the Lutheran Church today must oppose the modern theories that this only has to do with the church holding up the unique sacrifice of Calvary before the Father. The Roman sacrifice of the Mass is more than this according to the teaching of the Council of Trent (Session 22), that is, a truly atoning sacrifice in itself, however its relationship to the sacrifice of the cross may be defined (*instauratio, repraesentatio*, etc.).

In contrast to Calvin, who saw in the doctrine of transubstantiation the real cause for the decline of the Biblical Lord's Supper and the root of all corruption (which is historically untenable, since the doctrine of transubstantiation is over a millennium younger than the doctrine of the sacrifice of the Mass), Luther judged this teaching relatively mildly. For him it was a philosophical aberration of theology, a "clever sophistry," which does not agree with the statements of Scripture, in which the consecrated bread is still called bread (SA III VI; cf. 1 Cor. 10:16; 11:28). He judged the doctrine of concomitance even more mildly: "We need not resort to the specious learning of the sophists and the Council of Constance that as much is included under one form as under both. Even if it were true that as much is included under one form as under both, yet administration in one form is not the whole order and institution as it was established and commanded by Christ."

Luther also clearly recognized the danger that threatens every theologian, that he might follow not only Scripture as the *norma normans* but also some philosophy, whether it be Aristotelian-Thomistic, which seeks to explain the miracle of the Lord's Supper with the philosophical miracle of transubstantiation, or the Platonic-Neoplatonic theory of image and sign, which since the days of Augustine was the great danger for the church and which was revived by Zwingli and Calvin, each in his own way. He also faced the temptation, which captured Zwingli, to understand the Words of Institution figuratively, the *est* in the sense of *significat*. He knew that there could be no stronger weapon against the Roman Church than if one could prove that the Words of Institution must be understood in this sense. However, he withstood this philosophical temptation, which also had implications for church politics: "The text is too powerfully present" [WA 15:394; American Edition 40:68]. He also withstood the final and most difficult temptation to sacrifice the complete irrationality of the miracle of the Lord's Supper for Zwingli's humanistic-rationalistic objection: *Deus non proponit nobis incomprehensibilia* (God does not put incomprehensible statements before us). On the contrary, thought Luther, all the great truths of the Christian faith are *incomprehensibilia!* He here rightly recognized that the rationalizing of the doctrine of the Lord's Supper brings with it the rationalizing of the whole dogma of the church.

However, it was not some kind of practical or theoretical considerations that led Luther to his doctrine of the Lord's Supper, but the Word of Scripture entirely alone. On the one hand, he saw the disagreement of all his opponents and their inability to offer a credible, cohesive interpretation of the Words of Institution. On the other, he saw the Word that no exegesis could shake: "This is My body."

> Consequently, you can boldly address Christ both in the hour of death and at the Last Judgment: "My dear Lord Jesus Christ, a controversy has arisen over thy words in the Supper. Some want them to be understood differently from their natural sense. But since they teach me nothing certain, but only lead me into confusion and uncertainty . . . I have remained with thy text as the words read. If there is anything obscure in them, it is because thou didst wish to leave it obscure, for thou hast given no other explanation of them, nor hast thou commanded any to be given. . . .
>
> If there should be anything obscure about these words, thou wilt bear with me if I do not completely understand them, just as thou didst forbear with thine apostles when they did not understand thee in many things—for instance, when thou didst announce thy passion and resurrection. And yet they kept thy words just as they were spoken and did not alter them. Thy beloved mother also did not understand when thou saidst to her, Luke 2 [:49], "I must be about my Father's business," yet with simplicity she kept these words in her heart and did not alter them. So have I also kept to these thy words. . . . Behold, no fanatic will dare to speak thus with Christ, as I know full well, for they are uncertain and at odds over their text. (WA 26:446f. [American Edition 37:305–06])

That is genuine theology that speaks when God's Word speaks and is silent when God's Word is silent.

3.

But, it is objected, one cannot ignore the progress of exegesis and the findings of four centuries of historical research. To that we have to answer that the Lutheran Church does not think of standing by the formulations of the 16th century without testing them. We certainly reserve the right not to consider the Bultmannian interpretation of the New Testament, just to mention the most prominent example of our time, as truly serious exegesis. According to it, Jesus did not regard Himself as the Christ at all, and the assertions about Him, such as the One born of the Virgin Mary, the Lamb of God, who bears the sins of the world, His resurrection and ascension, are considered to be myths. We do not even take this interpretation seriously as historical scholarship.

Genuine historical scholarship we take very seriously. It has pleased

God to reveal Himself in history and to give us the Holy Scriptures as the documents of a great history of salvation. But precisely on the question of Holy Communion one can study the possibility and the limit of the historical task.

There is no longer any serious historian who denies that Jesus instituted the Lord's Supper. Indeed, there are hardly any scholars who seriously deny that Jesus wished this Supper to be repeated by His people. Where in early Christendom would there have been the commanding spirit who would have thought of bridging the time between the death and the return of the Lord with such a celebration, in which past and future again and again become present, and the distance between heaven and earth is bridged? The church has been able to survive the delay of the Lord's return, for which it has been praying for 19 centuries and for which it has been waiting so long, only because Sunday after Sunday is the "Day of the Lord," the day of the anticipated parousia, the day on which He comes to His congregation under the lowly forms of bread and wine and "incorporates" Himself in it anew.

Christendom did not take this over from the Jews or from the Gentiles. Neither a congregation nor an individual contrived it, neither one of the original apostles nor Paul, who was so greatly suspect to the Jewish Christian congregations. What a weapon he would have provided for his enemies if anything unhistorical could have been found in what he reported in 1 Corinthians as a tradition about the Lord's Supper! He himself then would have fallen under the anathema of Gal. 1:8f. And what Christian of the first century could ever have come up with the idea of drinking blood, which was inconceivable to every Jewish spirit and would even have been intolerable if it was only intended symbolically. There is only One who possessed the authority for such an institution, and that was Jesus Himself.

The tradition about the Lord's Supper quoted by Paul in 1 Cor. 11:23ff. belongs to the bedrock of the tradition of the historical Jesus, which no criticism of a serious historian can destroy. That this tradition is good and reliable is confirmed by the mention of the fact that the cup was given "after supper," while Mark and Matthew are no longer interested in this not unimportant detail, which had not come into church usage even though it was mentioned in liturgical formulas following the example of Paul. Where is there anywhere in the history of religion of the ancient world a fact like the institution of the Lord's Supper by Jesus that is attested by two different traditions in different form (Paul-Luke and Mark-Matthew) but so consistent in substance?

Historical problems certainly still remain. The Aramaic wording of the words spoken by Jesus can only be reconstructed by conjecture, and the conjectures will always differ. The famous question of the relationship of the Johannine (and perhaps Pauline) dating of the Last Supper with the 13th or 14th of Nisan and with this the understanding of this Supper as an anticipatory or an actual Passover, a question with which the early Easter controversies are connected, cannot be decided with absolute certainty. And so here, as with so many questions of the life of Jesus, our natural curiosity, as well as the historian's legitimate thirst for knowledge, remains unsatisfied. Here also Holy Scripture proceeds as usual. It tells us *only* what we should know because it belongs to our salvation, but *that* it does tell us. And the great art of exegesis consists in weighing all the questions of historical research and thinking them through, making use of all the findings of history, and then saying to the historian where the boundary of his knowledge lies.

Every historian is in danger of wanting to understand the people with whom he is dealing psychologically, to enter into their situation internally and externally, and from there to interpret their words. It is one of the basic realizations of recent theology that this procedure is not possible with the person of Jesus, and that is because our sources are not sufficient. The theologian will see in the extraordinary reserve of the evangelists, which makes a biography of Jesus and a description of His soul impossible, the indication that we cannot understand the God-Man psychologically. None of us can experience what went on in the soul of Jesus in the hour of the Last Supper. Thus all efforts to experience psychologically and to describe what Jesus must have been thinking at that time and how His words must therefore be explained are frustrated. That explains the diversity of the explanations, which Luther already criticized in those who felt they had to go behind the plain literal sense.

All we have are the Words of Institution as they have been transmitted in the New Testament in Greek translation in differing forms but with a consistent meaning. Jesus really meant what He said: that the bread that He gave to His disciples was His body. He really meant what He said: that the wine that He gave them in the cup was His blood. It cannot have been a parable, or he would have given an explanation or introduced it as a parable. In reality, He would have proposed a riddle for them instead of a parable, which no one has solved to this day. Even the appeal to the Pauline figure of speech of the "partaking of the body" and to the cup as a testament does not help us over the fact that Paul, as well as John, knows of an eating of the body (or flesh) and of a drinking of the blood. One also cannot give a new interpretation to "body," for the Johannine "flesh" shows what is meant. One cannot spiritualize "body" and "flesh." The "blood" stands there too. One cannot say that "flesh and blood" or "body and blood" together mean "person," for in the institution body and blood did not even appear in the same sentence. They appear in two sentences that were spoken at the beginning and at the end ("after supper") of the meal, separated by at least an hour.

One can say confidently that in the four centuries since Luther just about every conceivable path has been followed to get around the literal sense. At the end of this path of so much toil and trouble, of so much expenditure of powers of discernment and learning modern exegesis must capitulate before the plain wording. "The text stands there too powerfully." "The path of the spirit is the detour," said Hegel. From the detour of historical, psychological, and philosophical researches, discoveries, mistakes, and wrong tracks of so many centuries theology returns, insofar as it is genuine theology, to the paradoxical doctrine of the presence of the true body and blood of Christ in the Lord's Supper, to the Real Presence.

4.

This naturally is not to say that the exegesis of the future will come with flying colors into the camp of the Lutheran dogma of the Lord's Supper. This will not happen because this particular dogma is connected with the totality of Lutheran doctrine. But it will certainly happen that Luther will again be regarded as a serious "dialog partner." It will happen in this case also, as it has happened so often in the history of dogma: A defeated army will take over something from the victorious one and then claim the victory for itself. Zwingli's doctrine of the Lord's Supper has already been severely compromised in the Reformed Church. No one really wants to be a Zwinglian any more, just as even Calvin, in spite of the Consensus Tigurinus, thought he stood closer to Luther than to the Zurich reformer. If all the signs do not deceive, modern Calvinism is about to more or less give up Calvin's doctrine of the Lord's Supper. The *significat* of the Swiss reformers has very few friends left in the world, perhaps more among modern Lutherans than among theologically trained Reformed. But that does not mean a transition to the Lutheran doctrine. The great rock of offense remains the "materialistic" wording of the doctrine of the Lord's Supper of Luther and the Lutheran Church. Melanchthon, and the later Melanchthon at that, who had given up the "materialistic" wording of the Real Presence in favor of a "personal" one, seems to have become the church father of modern Protestantism in this respect.

There is an eclecticism in the making in the doctrine of the Lord's Supper that rejects Zwingli's and Calvin's spatial conception of heaven but at the same time rejects Luther's doctrine of the *unio sacramentalis*, the sacramental unity of the body and blood of Christ with the elements, and with it the oral reception of the body and blood of Christ and the reception by unbelievers. Christ in the midst of His congregation, His real presence understood in the sense of Matt. 18:20—that seems to be the winning solution to the question of the Lord's Supper toward which one aims, apparently a compromise in which Luther's concern is taken into account, but which in reality is a reformulation of Calvin's doctrine, from which certain time-bound ideas about the world and heaven have been abandoned. It is a solution that has made an impression on congregations and pastors, and yet it is a solution that is not consistent with Scripture, because Jesus did not at all say, "This is Myself," but "This is My body" and "This is My blood of the covenant."

Perhaps never has a more dangerous enemy of the Lutheran doctrine of the Lord's Supper appeared than this pure crypto-Calvinism. It is dangerous because this time it has taken hold not only of Electoral Saxony but of a great part of world Lutheranism. It is dangerous because there is scarcely a Lutheran church leader—with or without a bishop's cross—who grasps its theological significance. It is dangerous because the modern Lutheran Church no longer seems to know how to wield the weapon that alone can overcome this opponent: the Scriptural witness of the "It is written." Here lies fundamental reason why the Formula of Concord is today coming under such heavy attack. In it Luther's doctrine of the Lord's Supper is formulated in such a way that one cannot give it a new interpretation.

5.

A whole series of important questions could still be discussed here, but there is not enough space for this time. It should just be suggested that the principle of speaking when God's Word speaks and remaining silent when God's Word is silent should also consistently be brought into play when we speak of the purpose and use of the Sacrament of the Altar.

The church of the *sola scriptura* can never forget that the Lord's Supper is also a memorial meal. "This do in remembrance of Me." Has any of the great men of world history ever established such a memorial for himself as Jesus in His Supper? Has there ever been a testament as faithfully carried out as this one? "For the forgiveness of sins"? Has a church ever more faithfully preserved this than the church of the *sola fide*? According to Roman doctrine no one may receive Communion who is in a state of mortal sin, for with such a person, as Thomas (*S. th.* 3. 79. 3) explains, Christ cannot unite. Lutheran doctrine believes that Jesus comes only to such people, for He is the Savior of sinners.

Against the foolish objection that already before the Communion we receive forgiveness in the absolution Luther has already said what is necessary. We cannot receive forgiveness often enough and should receive it in all kinds of ways, for we remain sinners until we die, even though in faith we are righteous.

And finally concerning the connection between the Lord's Supper and the resurrection, which Luther loved to emphasize, he never went beyond what the Biblical teaching is. He knows the fact of the connection but not the how. One may not burden him with certain theosophical speculations of the 19th century about this how. Here too he speaks as Scripture speaks and is silent when Scripture is silent.

And if one reproaches him for dealing too briefly with the idea of the fellowship meal, the *synaxis*, then one has never read his sermons on the Lord's Supper, where the early Christian ideas about the bread made of many grains and the wine pressed from many grapes are found. Whether the Lutheran Church since then has guarded all these thoughts of the Reformer with sufficient care is another question.

Our task, dear brothers, is to stir them up again and to practice that great "instruction" that Article 24 of the Augsburg Confession requires of us. Let me, in conclusion, say a word about that.

Our first task is to celebrate the Sacrament of the Altar again and again quite seriously but also with the blessed joy of the first Christians (Acts 2:47). Moreover, we Lutherans have the great freedom that exists, as was already mentioned, in the celebration of the Roman Mass. It can take place in utter simplicity but also with the full splendor of the ancient liturgy of the Lord's Supper, which Luther preserved and the Lutheran Church kept for two centuries with such great love as a priceless treasure.

That's where the "instruction" comes in. Here we can learn from the liturgical movement of our time. On this point they are clearly right.

Our people should know the meaning of the Gloria, the Preface, the Sanctus, the Benedictus and Hosanna, the Consecration as it is expounded in the Formula of Concord, the Agnus Dei, and the Communion. We can explain it to them in special lectures, but we can also do it in sermon and Bible class. So many texts emerge totally spontaneously: the great types of the Lord's Supper in the Old Testament—Melchizedek, the sacrifice of Isaac, the Passover, manna, the miraculous feeding of Elijah exhausted to the dropping point in the wilderness. Then in the New Testament, besides the specific texts of the Lord's Supper, there are all the parables and other sayings of the Lord that speak about the future messianic banquet, the Passion history together with the farewell discourses, the first church, the liturgical formulas in the epistles and in Revelation, everything that speaks of the church, and all texts about the high priestly and kingly office of Christ.

What totally new substance our confirmation instruction would receive if it again became sacramental instruction and the Fourth and Sixth Chief Parts did not just make up a more or less unrelated appendage. And don't let anyone come up with the excuse that the children are not yet mature enough or that they would misunderstand it. Where that sort of thing is said, it may be assumed that the teacher is not yet mature enough. How one can say these things to children one can learn, with the necessary changes, from the Catholic instruction for First Communion. That is what we can do. The rest God must do: awaken the hunger and thirst for the Sacrament, which is always at the same time a hunger and thirst for the Word of God.

Something else also belongs in our instruction of the congregation about the Sacrament of the Altar according to Article 24 of the Augsburg Confession: "The people are also given instruction about other false teaching concerning the sacrament." That is not to be avoided. The condemnations cannot be separated from the positive explanation of the doctrine. Even in Barmen one can not get away from this, although one might try to ignore the Scriptural condemnations of false doctrine in the Confessions of the Reformation. The "damnamus" is not a loveless judgment against other Christians but the rejection of false doctrine that is commanded in the New Testament, a duty of pastoral care for those who are straying no less than for those who are endangered by error. If our church right at this point has always taken this most seriously and has not admitted to the Lutheran celebration of the Lord's Supper those who reject the Lutheran doctrine of the Sacrament, it has not thereby anticipated the Last Judgment. In the ancient church the communicant, to whom the consecrated elements were given with the words "The body of Christ" and "The blood of Christ," answered with his "Amen." How can one who is Reformed say Amen to the Lutheran distribution formula? He must take offense at it. Who gives us the right to mislead someone into an unworthy reception of the Lord's Supper in that he does not discern the body of the Lord (1 Cor. 11:29), and to whom would we want to be accountable for it? Is that Christian love?

We must be clear about the fact that there is a profound difference in the understanding of the Lord's Supper here. Not only is the meaning of the Words of Institution in dispute between Lutherans and Reformed, but from this difference also emerges a totally different understanding of the practice of the Lord's Supper. The Lord's Supper can and must have a different purpose in the Reformed Church than among Lutherans. It can and must, as a human act of confession, become a means toward union. That is what it has become in the Reformed and in the crypto-Calvinistic churches of our day. While for us Lutherans—just as for the Catholic churches of the East and West—the Sacrament of the Altar can only be the goal of unification, it stands firm for all Reformed churches and those churches influenced by the Reformed spirit that it is the *means* of unification that Christ willed.

Therefore the idea in the "Constitution of the Evangelical Church in Germany," specially provided for the sake of a few backward Lutherans but completely clear in its meaning, is that altar fellowship—which is basically the same as admission to the Lord's Supper—is the norm between all parts of this church. The legal restriction, practically speaking, is without any significance because this altar fellowship has been generally practiced in fact and in principle—and not just since the [constituting] Synod of Eisenach. The argument based on the need of the refugees is only an excuse, as is already shown by the fact that in the last century one used internal migration as the justification. Besides, there were hardly any Reformed in a number worth mentioning among the refugees from the East, and these have by now made contact with their mother church, at least insofar as they are religious.

Thus it is also claimed that at every churchly gathering today there must be a common celebration of the Lord's Supper, which then becomes the high point, the "unforgettable experience," for all participants at which one feels the breath of the Spirit and the presence of the Lord in a way that Zinzendorf would have been proud of.

As it is in Germany, so it is in the ecumenical realm. To be sure, at Amsterdam the concession of their own celebrations of the Lord's

Supper had to be made to the weak flesh of the Orthodox, the Anglo-Catholics, and the Lutherans, but with pride the enormous stride forward was reported in that a Scandinavian prelate participated in no less than three of the "Lord's Suppers," and Martin Niemöller announced *urbi et orbi* how this Lutheran archbishop had gone with him and the Archbishop of Sydney to the Reformed Lord's Supper, together with all manner of sectarians.

What is really the motive of such going to the Lord's Supper? Since when is the Lord's Supper a means of church politics in the Lutheran Church? What does the Christian congregation, which according to Luther is to judge doctrine, have to say to its bishops on this question? Does it have nothing at all to say any more? Then Western Christendom might just as well have spared itself the Reformation. And what does the Lord Christ say to all this? Now that is something everyone can look up in the second and third chapters of the Revelation of St. John.

In heartfelt affection I greet you, dear brothers in the ministry, in this jubilant season of the church year.

THE LUTHERAN UNDERSTANDING OF THE CONSECRATION

Letters to Lutheran Pastors, No. 26
July 1952

Dear Brothers in the Ministry!

Various inquiries from your circle suggest that I say a word about the Lutheran understanding of the consecration in Holy Communion. Among these was the question of a layman from the Prussian Free Church on how one is to understand the connection between the recommendation or introduction of the epiclesis and the withdrawal of the "for the forgiveness of sins" into the background in the recent liturgical movement. This was asserted in Letter 23 ("The Scriptural Basis of the Lutheran Doctrine of the Lord's Supper").

A further inducement came from the fact that the question about the essence of the consecration has become a main issue in the liturgical movement that is going through the Lutheran churches in America and has been the cause of considerable controversy (cf. the article "The Theology of the Consecration in the Lord's Supper" by G. Drach in *The Lutheran Outlook*, March 1952, and the quarrel between this publication and the *Una Sancta* of the circle around Dr. A. C. Piepkorn, St. Louis). It could hardly be otherwise. Nowhere do dogmatics and liturgics affect each other more profoundly than in the question of the nature and function of the consecration. The answer to this question makes quite clear whether the Lutheran doctrine of the Real Presence has been grasped or not.

1.

Let me begin with a word about the *liturgical movement* in the Lutheran Church. It is a part of a large movement that goes through all of Christendom and perhaps also touches humanity outside the church, as the political pseudoceremonies and pseudoliturgies of our time suggest. It came about, as its origin in the years just after the turn of the century indicates, with the end of the dominance of rank individualism and rationalism. Where the liturgical movement appeared in the churches, it had something revolutionary about it—not without good reason was it tied up with the youth movement in Germany. It was a kind of revolution when in Catholic churches suddenly the table [*mensa*] of the early church replaced the high altar, while at the same time in Presbyterian churches in Scotland the Reformed communion table gave way to the medieval high altar. So church governments, from the Pope to Methodist church assemblies, had much trouble, the salutary kind of trouble that church governments need so that custom and thoughtlessness do not rule the church exclusively.

If one today in the middle of the century looks back to the results of the great movement, then one would have to say that only *one* church has dealt with it, has set aside its revolutionary excesses, and has put it in its service. That is the Roman Church, which in many countries, especially in Germany and Austria, derived a real inner renewal from this movement. This has happened. The fruits will only become completely clear when languages such as German and English have been raised to the level of liturgical languages and when a Catholic "German Mass" [*Deutsche Messe*] will remind Lutheranism that it was once a "German Mass" that led the Lutheran Reformation to victory. If one compares the success of the liturgical movement in the Roman Church with the failure of all efforts to renew the liturgical life of the evangelical churches in our time, one could have serious concerns about the future of these churches.

Where does the difference lie? What is evident immediately is that the liturgical movement in the Roman Church affected all of the people from the Catholic scholars to the most unsophisticated country congregations. All efforts on the Protestant side remain limited to pastors, some church-minded lay people, and very small, sometimes almost sectlike associations. The second immediately obvious difference is that the liturgical movement in the Roman Church has remained on the foundations of Roman dogma in spite of some difficult conflicts with dogma and church order—it happened that liturgical scholars out of genuine

114

enthusiasm for its liturgy joined the Eastern Church—while on the other hand the liturgical movement in the area of the evangelical churches of Germany, including the Lutheran, has lived in continuous conflict with the church's confession. This has been all the more ominous since, besides the liturgical movement, the confessional movement in which Lutherans and Reformed were beginning to discover anew the confession of the Reformation and the doctrine of the church had been going on since the twenties. That this confessional movement has scarcely any relationship with the liturgy is in part to be explained by the fact that it received the strongest impulses from the Reformed side. Karl Barth has never understood what church liturgy is, and how should he ever know it! On the other hand, leaders of the liturgical movement were men who had never experienced the rediscovery of the Reformation and the doctrine of the church: Heiler, whose supposed conversion to Lutheranism in Uppsala was a misunderstanding, as though revolt against the Pope were already Lutheranism, and Wilhelm Stählin, who came from the Nuremberg church, influenced by Melanchthon and the Enlightenment, and from the Gnostic movement of Rudolf Steiner's "Anthroposophy." It is significant that these two men have never understood the *sola fide*. For Heiler the authentic doctrine of justification has always been that of Trent, while Stählin is a latter-day disciple of Osiander. He has always dismissed the doctrine of justification in the Formula of Concord with strong words, even though his literary statements are somewhat more cautious. One should read over his book, *Vom göttlichen Geheimnis* (1936), now translated into English [*The Divine Mystery*], putting the question, What happens here to the basic doctrines of the Reformation? His criticism of the doctrine of forensic justification, p. 67 [106], no longer leaves any room for the idea that God's forgiving and absolving verdict is our righteousness. That we have no other righteousness than the righteousness of Christ, that our righteousness is always an alien righteousness—this humbling and gladdening truth no longer has a place in a theology that regards man's "transformation" as his redemption. As a result, the *sola fide* disappears. This book speaks of faith only in the sense of the devout appropriation of the divine mystery, no longer in the sense of confidence [*fiducia*] in God's mercy in Christ. *Sola scriptura* also disappears. What's the good of all the beautiful words about the "mystery of the Word," pp. 32ff. [55ff.], and about the character of the Bible as revelation if there are also additional sources of revelation, tradition and the mystical experience? Or is it not the Catholic tradition out of which it can be said about the sacraments among Lutherans: "What we in the Evangelical Church call 'Sacraments' is all that is still left from a world of mystery that once embraced and filled the whole life of the Christian Church in its breadth, length, depth and height" (p. 49 [79])? And what else is that "meditation," without which we cannot grasp the depths of a Bible passage or other matters, than a Gnostic-mystical experience ("How does one achieve knowledge of higher worlds?" as we are reminded of Steiner's book)? Not the straightforward hearing of the Word with the assistance of the Holy Spirit but "meditation" should disclose "the divine secret" to the person. So we hear that "practice in meditation is an inestimable aid to really hearing the word, to penetrating into the secret meaning of a Bible phrase, or to experiencing in ourselves the power of a sign or of a melody" (p. 75 [118]). What a combination: Bible, sign, melody!

> All meditation originates a union, perhaps not to be dissolved, between my psychical experience and certain spiritual contents, words, pictures, signs. Every genuine meditative experience is conscious of that very strange occurrence, that I become one with the object contemplated, not so that I pass over to it, but rather that it comes to me, pulls me by the body; indeed, enters into myself so that I experience its presence even in bodily sensations. (p. 75 [117])

This meditation, whose origin from Gnostic sects is well known, should find its "most beautiful example" in what the Christmas story tells of Mary: "She kept all these things, pondering them in her heart" (p. 75 [118]). To that is added: "Luther often pointed to this." Really? He certainly did not mean this "meditative experience." He spoke in another way about the Word, about faith, and about the Holy Spirit, who works in us faith in the Word.

It is an unspeakable tragedy of German Protestantism that behind such out and out pathological and heretical movements there was a genuine longing for the renewal of the Lutheran liturgy and the sacraments in line with the Lutheran Church. It is this yearning that has led so many Lutherans in Germany into the High Church movement, above all that of the Berneuchener. Here they thought they could find what was no longer offered in the churches that no longer understood their own liturgy, neglected the prayer of the church, the daily prayer, and let the Sacrament of the Altar deteriorate. From this one must understand the success of the Berneuchener. They did something. They did much that was wrong, but at least they acted. And who would deny that they have also accomplished something good in the area of liturgical prayer and authentic church music? This is the reason that W. Stählin also enjoys respect among those who object to him theologically. But it remains a tragedy of the German church in the past generation that the confessional movement and the liturgical movement did not find the way to each other.

Confession and liturgy belong inseparably together if the church is to be healthy. Liturgy is prayed dogma; dogma is the doctrinal content of the liturgy. The placement of liturgy above dogma, for which one calls in the liturgical movements of all confessions with the well-known saying "lex orandi lex credendi" [the law of what is to be prayed is the law of what is to be believed] ("ut legem credendi lex statuat supplicandi," Celestine I, Denzinger 139, called to remembrance by Pius XI in "Divini Cultus," Denz. 2200), has been opposed in the Roman Church by the present Pope [Pius XII] in his encyclical "Mediator Dei," in which he points out that one can also turn this saying around and that in all circumstances dogma should be the norm for the liturgy. If that is already known in Rome, how much more should it be known in the church that makes or would like to make the right understanding of the Gospel also be the criterion for the liturgy.

We Lutherans know nothing of liturgy that is prescribed by God's Word. We know that the church has freedom to order its ceremonies and that it can therefore preserve the liturgical heritage of Christendom, as long as it is consistent with the Gospel. Indeed, our church in the Reformation placed the greatest value on preserving as much as possible this heritage that binds us with the fathers. But these ceremonies do not belong to the essence of the church or to the true unity of the church, as Article 7 of the Augsburg Confession and Article 10 of the Formula of Concord teach. Löhe knew this when in his *Drei Bücher von der Kirche* [*Three Books on the Church*], right where he speaks of the beauty and greatness of the Lutheran liturgy, he protests against overestimating it: "The church remains what she is even without liturgy. She remains a queen even when she is dressed as a beggar" (Book 3, chap. 9 [p. 178]). Even the Pope has reminded his bishops that the Masses that are secretly celebrated in prison camps, without any pomp, in utter simplicity, come very near to the Mass of the ancient church and are not inferior to a pontifical Mass. In Lutheran Germany, however, one can today hear theologians—even some who come from unliturgical Württemberg—say that there is a form of the divine service that belongs to the essence of the church, even that Gregorian chant belongs essentially to the Christian liturgy. It is high time that the liturgical movement in the Lutheran church wakes up from its romantic dreams and subordinates itself to the norms to which the whole life of the church must be subject: the *norma normans* of Holy Scripture and the *norma normata* of the church's confession. And this applies to all the Lutheran churches in the world, for the Scandinavian, in which the Anglican influence is so great, and for the American, in which the ideas of the European liturgical movement have now gained a footing. If this serious reflection does not take place, then the liturgical movement will become what it has become already for many of its adherents: the end of Lutheranism and the road to Rome.

2.

On one point the liturgical movement is right absolutely without a doubt, and here it is irrefutable. It has called attention to the fact that the Lutheran Church has more or less gone the way of Reformed Protestantism in being without the Sacrament, and thereby it has lost what belongs to the essence of the Lutheran Church. A part of the essence of the church in the Lutheran sense is the *Sacrament*, and that in a different sense than the Reformed Church claims that about itself. Lutherans and Reformed do not mean the same thing when they use the word "sacrament." For the Reformed sacrament is always only a sign of divine grace, a sign that can remain empty, that is, when it might please God to have it so, a sign of a grace that also exists without the sign. They are actions that Christ has commanded and that man must carry out; by fulfilling them we show our obedience to the Lord of the church. For Lutherans sacrament is more than a sign; it is a means of grace in the strict sense. In Baptism we receive the forgiveness of sins, rebirth, and the gift of the Holy Spirit, no matter what we may do with this grace later. In Holy Communion we actually receive with the mouth the body and blood of our Lord for the forgiveness of sins or, if we do not believe this, to our judgment.

This difference in the understanding of sacrament, however, must also work itself out in the celebration of a sacrament. So in the Reformed church every divine service is a "sacramental divine service" [*Sakramentsgottesdienst*] in which one of the two sacraments that exist according to Reformed belief is celebrated, either Baptism or the Lord's Supper. What matters is that the congregation carries out Christ's command. This explains the remarkable custom in modern Reformed churches of performing baptism before the assembled congregation in the divine service. This is probably an influence of the Baptist churches, where the baptismal tank replaces the altar and baptism is performed as an actual bath with as much water as possible, so that the poor person being baptized has to rush out of the church in order to change clothes on the outside.

The early church did it just the other way around. It had the baptism performed outside in front of the church by the deacon—just as the apostles themselves seldom baptized but entrusted it to their helpers (Acts 10:48; 1 Cor. 1:14ff.)—after which the newly baptized came into the church. For this reason the baptismal font according to ancient custom had its place at the entrance of the church. If it were not so hopelessly dreary to witness the thoughtlessness and ignorance of modern Lutheranism, one could smile over the eagerness with which the German and American Lutherans are now also taking over the custom of performing baptism in the congregational divine service—which from experience is thereby interrupted—from the Reformed churches. The Rhenish Church, the most Reformed among the provincial churches of the Old Prussian Union, has elevated this custom or nuisance [*Sitte oder Unsitte*]—it depends entirely on the outlook—to the level of church law. That is the same church in which, despite the Union, despite Barmen, despite the EKiD [Evangelische Kirche in Deutschland]—in which according to its constitution one should "listen to the testimony of the brothers"—one controversy over candles after another broke out because the Lutherans want to have their candles on the altar and the Reformed forbid them because they are not necessary for salvation, as W. Niesel was not ashamed to report in the Reformed church paper.

Naturally, the question of the place of the baptismal font and the time of day at which baptism is performed, as well as the question of the size of the congregation that is present, is just as much an adiaphoron as the question of whether and how many candles should burn on the altar. The Lutheran Church has the freedom to transfer baptism into the divine service, provided it would not be the occasion to smuggle the Reformed concept of sacrament into our congregations, as if Baptism were a sign that must be seen by as many spectators as possible, a sign that we men may discard, and not the means of grace through which a human soul is born again to eternal life. The instant the Lutheran congregations, as in the Rhineland, have to submit to a Reformed law, the new custom ceases to be an adiaphoron. Then the *casus confessionis* exists, in which there is no more adiaphoron according to Article 10 of the Formula of Concord.

But assuming that the *casus confessionis* does not exist and that our church, in the exercise of the freedom that it has in all matters of ceremony, introduces baptism into the divine service, this service would not thereby become, as Karl Barth thinks, a sacramental worship service [*Sakramentsgottesdienst*]. The only sacramental worship service in the Lutheran sense is the divine service in which the Sacrament that belongs in the Sunday divine service is celebrated, *Holy Communion*. For the Lord's Supper is still for Luther simply "the Sacrament," as his usage that again and again puts "Baptism and the Sacrament" together shows (e.g., in the Short Preface to the Large Catechism, Müller, [*Die symbolischen Bücher der evangelisch-lutherischen Kirche*], 380: "yet they come to Baptism and the Sacrament and exercise all the rights of Christians, although those who come to the Sacrament ought to know more . . ." [LC Pref 5]). Others follow him in this, e.g., Justus Jonas in the translation of the Apology (at AC VII/VIII, Müller, 154: "they have one and the same Baptism and Sacrament," which corresponds to the Latin text: *habent . . . eadem sacramenta*).

As is well known, the term "sacrament" is never totally precisely defined in the Lutheran Confessions, and that is because the concept of sacrament is not found in Holy Scripture and is only a way of thinking of later theology in order to summarize the actions instituted by Christ (Baptism, Lord's Supper, Office of the Keys) into categories. Lutherans should never have gotten involved in the polemics regarding the vacillation of the confessions on the question of what all are sacraments. Christ did not institute "the sacraments" but each particular rite. Whether one calls absolution—which does not exist in the Reformed church—sacrament or Gospel is a question of terminology and nothing more. Among these rites, however, is one that belongs to the divine service, without which there is no proper Sunday divine service in the church of the New Testament and in the Lutheran Church of the 16th and 17th centuries, even though Holy Scripture lays down no law about when and how often the command of Jesus, "Do this . . ." (Luke 22:19f.; 1 Cor. 11:24f.), should be followed. This is what the fathers of the early church called the sacrament of sacraments [*sacramentum sacramentorum*] and what Luther simply called "the Sacrament," the Sacrament of the Altar. To restore this Sacrament, which under the influence of Reformed Protestantism and the modern world has also declined in Lutheranism, and give it its proper place in the divine service dare not be an interest only of a liturgical reform movement. It is a matter of life and death for the Lutheran Church.

3.

Among the great teachers of the church there has probably been none who has understood the inner connection of *Word and Sacrament,* of *Gospel and the Lord's Supper* as profoundly as Martin Luther. The church, of course, has always known that the means of grace belong together and thus far form a unity. It is very remarkable that even for Catholicism it is the Word added to the element that first makes the sacrament a sacrament. The Word is the *forma* without which the *materia* can never be a sacrament. But what Roman dogmatics has never seen is the connection between the Sacrament of the Altar and the proclamation of the Gospel. If it had understood this, there would never have been the neglect of the sermon, which even there remains a mark of Catholicism, where one has outstanding preachers and the obligation of preaching every Sunday is impressed on the priests. In the Catholic sacrament of Ordination the priestly office, the authority to offer the sacrifice of the Mass for the living and the dead, and the Office of the Keys, authority to forgive sins, are conveyed, but not the authority to proclaim the Gospel. Now to be sure Holy Communion is a particular form of the proclamation of the Gospel ("For as often as you eat this bread and drink the cup, you proclaim the Lord's death until He comes" 1 Cor. 11:26), but it is not the only way.

The Lord's Supper without the sermon would be a misunderstood rite, just as the sermon, if it were not regularly accompanied by the Lord's Supper as our Lord instituted it, would very soon cease to be proclamation of the Gospel. Those are statements that the experience of Christendom confirms. An Abyssinian Mass and a preaching service in many a prominent, modern Protestant church in New York have in common that they are religious ceremonies from which one can no longer hear the Gospel of the crucified and returning Lord. Before this fact all other differences for theology fade away.

For the Crucified One becomes a figure of the past if His true body and His true blood, what He sacrificed for our sins on Golgotha, are not present in the Sacrament of the Altar and given to us. And the One who is coming again becomes a figure of a distant, unforeseeable future that lies beyond the scope of our life unless the church's prayer, "Maranatha," "Come, Lord Jesus," is already fulfilled now in every celebration of the Lord's Supper. There is no Gospel without the Real Presence. *The Lord's Supper is a component of the Gospel; the Gospel is the content of the Lord's Supper.* That is what Luther saw. Therefore for him the struggle for the Gospel was at the same time the struggle for the Sacrament of the Altar.

The connection between the Gospel and Lord's Supper becomes perfectly clear in the Lutheran doctrine of the *consecration*, as it is fully set forth in Article 7 of the Solid Declaration § 73ff. (Müller, 663ff.). There the decisive sentences state:

No man's word or work, be it the merit or the speaking of the minister, be it the eating and drinking or the faith of the communicants, can effect the true presence of the body and blood of Christ in the Supper. This is to be ascribed only to the almighty power of God and the Word, institution, and ordinance of our Lord Jesus Christ. For the truthful and almighty words of Jesus Christ which he spoke in the first institution were not only efficacious in the first Supper but they still retain their validity and efficacious power in all places where the Supper is observed according to Christ's institution and where his words are used, and the body and blood of Christ are truly present, distributed, and received [*corpus et sanguis Christi vera praesentia distribuantur et sumantur*] by the virtue and potency of the same words which Christ spoke in the first Supper. For wherever we observe his institution and speak his words over the bread and the cup and distribute the blessed bread and cup, Christ himself is still active through the spoken words by the virtue of the first institution, which he wants to be repeated. Chrysostom says in his *Sermon on the Passion:* "Christ himself prepares this table and blesses it. No human being, but only Christ himself who was crucified for us, can make of the bread and wine set before us the body and blood of Christ. The words are spoken by the mouth of the priest, but by God's power and grace through the words that he speaks, 'This is my body,' the elements set before us [*proposita elementa*] in the Supper are blessed. Just as the words, 'Be fruitful and multiply and fill the earth,' were spoken only once but are ever efficacious in nature and make things grow and multiply, so this word was spoken only once, but it is efficacious until this day, and until his return it brings it about that his true body and blood are present in the church's Supper [*usque ad hodiernum diem et usque ad eius adventum praestat sacrificio firmitatem*]." [FC SD VII 75–76]

4.

If one wants to understand these statements, one must comprehend what they have in common with *Roman doctrine* and what separates them from it. At first glance it might appear that the Roman Church is done an injustice here. Does it not also teach, referring to the fathers of the fourth century, above all Ambrose, but also referring to the word of Chrysostom in *De prod. Judae* 1. 6 (Migne *SG* 49:380), that the priest performs the consecration *ex persona Christi* and that it is not human words but the words of Christ that bring about the miracle of the Real Presence? In *Summa Th.* 3, q. 78, Thomas quotes the words of Ambrose from *De sacramentis:* "The consecration happens by the words and statements of the Lord Jesus" [*Consecratio fit verbis et sermonibus Domini Jesu*]; everything else that is said in the way of prayers is a human word and does not have the effect of Christ's words: "Therefore, what Christ says, this it is that makes the sacrament" [*Ergo sermo Christi hoc conficit sacramentum*] (Migne *SL* 16:440). Yes, even the comparison between the Words of Institution and the words of creation, as Chrysostom offers it, is readily repeated in Catholic dogmatics (cf. *Deutsche Thomas-Ausgabe* 30:429).

Are the fathers of the Formula of Concord, above all is Luther, who knew Roman doctrine well, not guilty of a sin against the Eighth Commandment when they contend that that church teaches consecration through the word of the priest? Could the Reformed not say the same thing about the Lutheran view of the consecration? What sort of basic difference exists for a strict Calvinist between the Catholic priest and the Lutheran pastor, who both maintain that the Words of Institution that they speak bring about the miracle of the Real Presence as the words of Christ?

In fact, the Lutheran doctrine has a true kinship here with the Catholic. It is no accident that the Formula of Concord here appeals to the teachers of the ancient church, who are the fathers for the Roman as well as the Lutheran Church. Both churches are churches of the Real Presence; both churches believe that in every valid Lord's Supper the same miracle takes place as at the first Lord's Supper and that then as now it is the Lord's Words of Institution [*verba testamenti*] that bring about this miracle of the Real Presence. And yet there is a profound contrast between them. Where does this contrast lie?

It does not lie, as many simply assume, in the question of *transubstantiation*. The doctrine of transubstantiation is condemned by Luther and the Lutheran Church because it is not consistent with Scripture—which speaks of the consecrated bread as still bread in 1 Cor. 11:26ff.—and therefore is a false philosophical-theological theory that tries to describe the miracle, which mocks every description and explanation. But the doctrine of transubstantiation does at least want to hold firmly to the Real Presence. For this reason Luther always judged it more mildly than the Enthusiasts' and the Zwinglians' denial of the Real Presence. In this matter, despite the deep chasm that exists, the Lutherans stand closer to Rome than to the Reformed, even to the Calvinists.

And one may not, as still happens, attribute a doctrine of consubstantiation to Lutheranism and try to understand the contrast on that basis. If Luther early in his career appealed to the consubstantiation taught by the Occamists against transubstantiation, he only did it to show that even within the Roman Church the doctrine of transubstantiation was not the only option. But the doctrine that two "substances" exist alongside each other, the substance of the bread and the substance of the body of Christ, is also a philosophical method of explanation, which is not the teaching of our church. Selnecker, the contributor to the Formula of Concord, protested explicitly against this misunderstanding when he wrote in 1591: "Even if our churches use the ancient little words that in the bread, with the bread, or under the bread the body of Christ is received, no *Inclusio* or *Consubstantiatio* or *Delitescentia*—inclusion, dual essence, or concealment—is thereby fabricated" (*Vom Heiligen Abendmahl des Herrn* [1591], fol. E2). And similar protests have been made again and again.

Even the "in, with, and under" with which the three expressions were later summarized is not a Lutheran doctrinal formulation. The prepositions "in," "with," and "under" are grammatical devices to express the miracle that the bread *is* the body and the wine *is* the blood. Everything depends on this *is* being maintained. For this reason the Lutheran Church did not criticize the old word "change" among the fathers. For *mutare*, which Melanchthon still cites in the quotation from Vulgarius (i.e., Theophylact, who in his commentary on Mark at 14:22 speaks of *metaballein*) in Article 10 of the Apology, is accepted as an expression of the ancient church and is not put on the same level with the Roman Church's *transsubstantiare*, which indeed it is not. That some had doubts about this is suggested by the omission of the quotation in the German translation of Justus Jonas as well as the translation of *metarrhythmizei* in the Chysostom quotation in the Formula of Concord with *consecrare*. Meanwhile, the Lutheran Church, although it rejected the doctrine of transubstantiation, has never found the primary catastrophic error in this or any other doctrine of change.

The antithesis lies at another point. Rome's error is not that the words of the consecration effect the Real Presence but that it understands the consecration as a sacrifice. Here, in the doctrine of the *sacrifice of the Mass*, not in the doctrine of transubstantiation, lies the grievous error that devastates the church for Luther. This is clear from a comparison between the article on the Mass in Part 2 and the article on the Sacrament of the Altar in Part 3 of the Smalcald Articles. "The Mass in the papacy must be regarded as the greatest and most horrible abomination because it runs into direct and violent conflict with this fundamental article"—that is, the *articulus stantis et cadentis ecclesiae* [the office and work of Jesus Christ and our redemption]. "Yet, above and beyond all others, it has been the supreme and most precious of the papal idolatries" (SA II II; Müller, 301). That was from the beginning of the Reformation until the end of his life the conviction of the same man for whom transubstantiation was a "clever sophistry," a false speculation contrary to Scripture. Luther did not impute guilt to himself for the fact that he had believed in this theory when he was a monk but for the fact that for 15 years he had said private Masses almost every day and thereby had committed idolatry "and worshiped not Christ's body and blood but only bread and wine and held them up for others to worship" (WA 38:197). That was one of the most severe anxieties of his life. That the sacrifice of the Mass, the most holy rite not only of the Roman Church but of all the churches of the East, the center of Christian piety for so many centuries, should be a violation of the First Commandment! One must understand this in order to comprehend the deep chasm between the Lutheran Lord's Supper and the Catholic Eucharist, between the Lutheran and the Roman Mass, between the Lutheran and Roman understanding of the consecration.

What does it mean that the Mass is a *sacrifice?* Already quite early, perhaps already at the end of the first century, the Eucharist was called a sacrifice, even though the New Testament significantly did not adopt this usage. For the comparison between the Lord's Supper and the sacrificial meals of the Jews and the Gentiles in 1 Cor. 10:18ff. says nothing more than that the Lord's Supper is a sacrificial *meal* in which we receive what Christ once sacrificed for us on the cross. Heb. 13:10 also says no more if one wishes to apply the verse to the Lord's Supper, as Catholic theology does.

The New Testament knows of the sacrifices of Christians, the *spiritual sacrifices* (1 Pet. 2:5) of praise and thanksgiving and of confession (Heb. 13:15), of the *koinonia* of the gifts of love (13:16), of the surrender of one's whole life in the service of God (Rom. 12:1). Generally here the word *sacrifice* is used in a figurative sense according to the pattern of Old Testament usage (e. g., Psalm 50:14; 51:19).

When one considers that Christianity, as a religion that did not involve the offering of sacrifices, came into a world of religions that did offer sacrifice, that the Christians were accustomed to sacrifice and the Jewish Christians in Jerusalem still participated in the sacrificial worship as long as there was a temple, then one can probably understand that they sought a replacement for the sacrifices that men do and found it above all in the prayer of praise and thanksgiving. So it was with the Jews of the diaspora and with all Judaism after the catastrophe of the year 70. Was it then such a big step to speak of the Eucharist, the church's great prayer of thanksgiving, also as a sacrifice?

In his great controversy with Trent, Martin Chemnitz answers the question of whether one may call the Lord's Supper a sacrifice in this figurative sense in the affirmative. But a limit is placed on this designation. The moment the Lord's Supper becomes an atoning sacrifice, then one has left the ground of the New Testament. For there we find only one sacrifice for sins: the sacrifice on Golgotha, which was offered once for all at a particular moment in history and is therefore unrepeatable and eternally valid. There in the New Testament there is only the high priesthood of Jesus and the priesthood of the whole people of God, the church (1 Peter 2:5, 9), of which every Christian is a member (Rev. 1:6). To this day no exegesis has been able to find there a distinctive priestly office besides the universal priesthood of all believers. The passage where the Roman Church believes it has found its priesthood, the office of the priest who offers the sacrifice of the Mass, is the words of our Lord at the Last Supper: "This do in remembrance of Me." Where is there anything about sacrifice there? Where is there even a hint that this was an ordination? How can one understand Jesus' command to repeat in such a way that from now on the apostles and the priests to be ordained by them should sacrifice the body and blood of our Lord for the living and the dead? Something is being read into the New Testament that is not there.

What is the novelty that has invaded the church with this notion of the priest who sacrifices the body and blood of our Lord? It is nothing else than what has found its expression in the idea of Mary, who as the second Eve takes her place beside the second Adam, participating in our Lord's work of redemption. It is nothing but the notion of man sharing in his redemption, a notion that has found its expression in the different types of the Catholic doctrine of grace in the East and West.

It is the claim that man has a part to play in what belongs to God alone. It is the secret pride [*superbia*] of man who cannot bear that he is dependent only on grace, only on the sacrifice that another offers for him, only on an "alien righteousness." This is the terrible tragedy of church history, which is not to be understood only as resulting from human error but from seduction by a superhuman power, that the holiest celebration of the church, in which Jesus Christ is present according to His divinity and humanity, has been ruined by the claim of man also to be something.

No beauty of the ancient liturgies can gloss over the fact that in them a human priest treads beside the eternal high priest, a sacrifice done by man beside Christ's sacrifice. None of the finely worked out theories about the identity of the sacrifice of the Mass with the sacrifice of the cross, e.g., Trent's idea that the Mass is a *repraesentatio* of the sacrifice on the cross, a making present of what happened once on Golgotha, eliminates the fact that in the Mass man is also offering a sacrifice: "We Your servants, but also Your holy people . . . offer to Your illustrious majesty . . . a holy victim, an immaculate victim" [*Nos servi tui, sed et plebs tua sancta . . . offerimus praeclarae majestati tuae . . . hostiam sanctam, hostiam immaculatam*]. Thus states the Canon of the Mass in the prayer that follows the prayer with the Words of Institution, and then God is asked graciously to accept the sacrifice as He did the sacrifices of Abel, Abraham, and Melchizedek. At the end of every Mass the priest implores the Holy Trinity "that the sacrifice that I, though unworthy, have offered before the eyes of Your majesty, may be acceptable to You, both for me and for all for whom I have offered it; may it move You to pity and *propitiate* You" [*ut sacrificium, quod oculis tuae majestatis indignus obtuli, tibi sit acceptabile, mihique et omnibus, pro quibus illud obtuli, sit te miserante propitiabile*]. Even if one stresses that the priest acts and speaks *ex persona Christi*, that in the sacrifice of the Mass Christ offers Himself to the Father and thus "re-presents" the sacrifice of the cross or makes it present, the fact remains that the priest makes the offering not only in the name of Christ but also in the name of the church, in the name of the faithful who are present, and even in his own name.

How can man take part in Christ's sacrifice? One must then go as far as modern Catholic theologians, who see in the sacrificing church the body of Christ, so that Christ and the church, the head and the body, do the sacrifice together. But then it is still a working together of God and man, and one even comes to a dangerous deification of man.

Concerning the relationship between the sacrifice of Golgotha and the church, Holy Scripture says: "Christ loved the church and gave Himself up for her, that He might sanctify her" (Eph. 5:25). It is characteristic of Catholic synergism that Mary under the cross is now no longer understood only as the church, for which Jesus died, but that the present Pope [Pius XII] in the conclusion of the encyclical *Mystici Corporis* can say of her that Mary also sacrificed her son there. In the doctrine of Mary as the "co-redemptrix" the final consequence of that synergism becomes clear that finds expression throughout the life and thought of Catholicism and also in the doctrine of the sacrifice of the Mass—the deification of man, the obliteration of the line between Creator and creature. This is what one comes to if one, in the words of Karl Adam, teaches "the wondrous fact that not only God but also creaturely powers—according to the conditional elements of their creatureliness— have a causative role in the work of redemption" (*Das Wesen des Katholizismus*, 6th ed. [1931], 141).

5.

Only from this profound contrast between the Roman Catholic view of the creature's cooperation in his redemption and the Reformation's conviction that there is no such cooperation and that *Christ alone* is the One "whom God made our wisdom, our righteousness and sanctification and redemption" [1 Cor. 1:30] can the difference in the understanding of the consecration be grasped. It is still true, despite every appeal to the word of Chrysostom and despite the contention that the priest speaks the consecration *ex persona Christi*, that he also still acts in his own name and in the name of the faithful. "We your servants, but also your holy people" offer to the Father the sacrifice of Christ's body and blood—not just the sacrifice of praise and thanksgiving, not just the gifts of the offertory. It is no accident that the Words of Institution are fitted into the prayers of the Canon of the Mass in the form of a relative clause and thereby become a part of a *human prayer*. However beautiful these Mass prayers may be, as not only the Roman Mass but also the liturgies of antiquity and of all the churches of the East have them, they remain human prayer and take the Words of Institution into human prayer. It is characteristic of the predominance of the human prayer that since the fourth century in the Eastern Church, the epiclesis, the invocation of the Holy Spirit to change the elements, has been understood as the actual consecration in place of the *verba testamenti* [Words of Institution]. But even if one, as was probably the case in the earlier Masses, understood the whole series of the prayers, including the Words of Institution, as the consecration, it would still be the prayer that consecrates. That is confirmed by the fact that in the Roman Mass the whole Canon is prayed inaudibly so that the congregation does not get to hear the Words of Institution and has to be alerted to the moment when they are spoken by the ringing of a bell. The elevation of the consecrated host for all practical purposes replaces the hearing of the Words of Institution. One must consider once what it meant for the German people, after over 700 years of Christian history, to hear the Words of Institution for the first time in the Lutheran Reformation, and that the same is true of the other nations who accepted the Reformation at that time. Then one will understand what the Lutheran Mass in the mother tongue meant for these peoples.

Long before he created this Mass after years of the most careful theological and liturgical work, *Luther* had recognized where the decisive error in Rome's understanding of the words of consecration lay. In *The Babylonian Captivity* he declared that what makes the Mass a proper Mass in the sense of the institution of Christ is the Word of Christ [*verbum Christi*] alone, i.e., the Words of Institution. "For in that word, and in that word alone, reside the power, the nature, and the whole substance of the mass" (*WA* 6:512 [American Edition 36:36]). Everything else is "accessory to the word of Christ" [*verbo Christi accessoria*]. A year later in *The Abolition of Private Masses* he interpreted the Words of Institution as the heart of the Sacrament of the Altar. In this Sacrament is the whole sum of the Gospel (*est enim in eo summa tota evangelii*, *WA* 8:447), as Paul says with the words: "As often as you eat of this bread and drink of this cup you will be proclaiming the Lord's death until He comes" (Luther is quoting the Vulgate). In the German version of the writing (*The Misuse of the Mass*) of the same year he says:

> For if you ask, What is the Gospel? you can give no better answer than these words of the New Testament, namely, that Christ gave his body and poured out his blood for us for the forgiveness of sins. This alone is to be preached to Christians, instilled into their hearts, and at all times faithfully commended to their memories. Thus the godless priests have made words of consecration out of them and concealed them so secretly that they would not reveal them to any Christian, no matter how holy and devout he has been. (*WA* 8:524 [American Edition 36:183])

Hidden deep in the Canon of the Mass among purely human prayers and in such a way that the Christian people can no longer hear them, the words of the Lord's Supper, the Gospel pure and simple, are stuck. By no longer permitting them to be heard and clothing them in human prayer formulas, they have made out of this Gospel a "benediction" [*Benedeiung*], a *verba consecrationis*, as the Latin wording says. That is, they have robbed the words of consecration of their real meaning. For in the Mass they are no longer good news to the believing sinner but only a consecration in the sense in which there are other consecrations, e.g., the consecration of churches or bishops, a rite of blessing with a particular effect. In view of all this we can understand why Luther, when he began to reform the Mass, immediately made two liturgical changes: The *words of the Lord's Supper* were to be chanted *aloud* by the liturgist, and the framing of Christ's words with a whole series of prayers was completely set aside. The only prayer that Luther left in this position was the *Lord's Prayer*, which in the Roman Mass follows the Canon, while Luther put it before the Words of Institution. For him no man-made prayer seemed tolerable beside the *verba testamenti*.

Theodor Knolle has shown the profound doctrinal and liturgical meaning of the old Lutheran Mass in several works (*Luther-Jahrbuch* [1928] and in his contribution to the volume *Vom Sakrament des Altars* [1941]) and raised a warning voice against the introduction of epicleses and eucharistic prayers, which bring the Words of Institution again into a relative clause between purely human words, even if they are beautiful and venerable human words. Even when one makes the utmost effort to speak of sacrifice only in an indisputably evangelical way, what is Lutheran still becomes a Roman Mass. The pious man again puts himself alongside Christ, and the Words of Institution are no longer the Gospel. The congregation edifies itself with its beautiful prayers, but it no longer hears the Gospel in the Lord's Supper. The forgiveness of sins recedes. It is no longer seen as the great and joyous gift of the Sacrament.

Is there some connection here with the fact that confession, which according to Lutheran teaching should precede the reception of the Sacrament of the Altar, is no longer taken very seriously? It is then either a General Confession without the complete seriousness of self-examination, which was a matter of course for our fathers, or it becomes in many High Church movements a poor imitation of the Roman auricular confession. But the deep inner connection that exists between absolution and the reception of the Sacrament is no longer understood. It can only be understood when one knows that both, *absolution and the Sacrament of the Altar*, are two sides of the same thing, that both are the *Gospel* for sinners. But if anyone wonders why we should receive forgiveness twice, what it means that one should be absolved of sins and then still receive the Sacrament for the forgiveness of sins, to such a one we may answer—Luther caught the spirit of it—"You have not yet pondered how great is the weight of sin."

6.

Although Luther understands the consecration in Holy Communion as something more than the consecration itself, more than the dedication of elements, it remains *consecration* in the strict sense. The Formula of Concord says it in this sense in its doctrine of consecration, as we quoted it above. It is the doctrine as our church developed it in the struggle against the Enthusiasts, after the doctrine of the consecration determined by the sacrifice of the Mass had been overcome in the struggle with Rome. Precisely because the Words of Institution may no longer in any way be blended with human words or be hidden among the words of men because they are the words of the Lord Christ Himself, they are as powerful as God's words in creation and accomplish what they say. So the Word of the Lord in every celebration of His Supper makes the bread to be the body and the wine to be the blood of the Lord. "For as soon as Christ says: 'This is my body,' His body is present through the Word and the power of the Holy Spirit" ("The Sacrament of the Body and Blood of Christ" [1526] *WA* 19:491 [American Edition 36:341]). "How that comes about you cannot know" (Ibid., 489 [340]). "We are not bidden to search out how it can be that our bread becomes and is the body of Christ" (*WA* 18:206 [American Edition 40:216]).

In accordance with the principle that theology should speak where God's Word speaks and should be silent where God's Word is silent, Luther and the Lutheran Confessions make no dogmatic statements about the how of the Real Presence. The philosophical lines of thought that are found here and there have a purely apologetic character. They do not try to explain the Real Presence but only to confront the reproach that the Lutheran doctrine is nonsense. *The Lutheran Church does not know a dogma about the how of the Real Presence that corresponds to transubstantiation.*

This restraint on the question of the how is also observed when it comes to dealing with *practical problems*. When does the Real Presence begin? When does it end? Is it limited to the moment of reception? What is the difference between a consecrated and an unconsecrated host? Is a second consecration necessary when the consecrated elements are not sufficient, and if so, why? What happens with the elements that are left over?

When one considers Luther's statements, one notices a very realistic "Catholicizing" attitude that is downright offensive to later Protestants of all confessions. First of all, it is determined that the Real Presence begins with the Words of Institution, which effect it. "There the words make the bread to be Christ's body given for us. Therefore it is no more just bread, but Christ's body wears the bread" [*Ergo non est amplius panis, sed corpus Christi hat das Brot an*] (*Sermon on the Catechism* [1528], *WA* 30/1:53). This notion is no different from the ideas of the *Formula Missae* (*WA* 12:214 [*LW* 53:30]) and the *Deutsche Messe* (*WA* 19:99 [*LW* 53:81]). It would "accord with the Lord's Supper to administer the sacrament immediately after the consecration of the bread, before the cup is blessed." For Luther is weighing whether it might not be best to follow Luke and Paul here. In this case the consecration would also remain a consecration and would not become a formula of distribution as has happened in many modern churches.

It is not necessary here to go into the fact that for Luther only the celebration of the Lord's Supper that corresponds to Christ's institution is a proper sacrament; therefore a private Mass in which no congregation communes is not one. The consecration spoken in this Mass is ineffective, while even in the Roman Mass with communion—even though only under one kind—Christ's institution is still there, though badly deformed. *Extra institutionem Christi* (outside of Christ's institution) the Sacrament is not there; consequently, the Real Presence ceases when the celebration is over. There is no reservation of the Sacrament, no procession with the Sacrament, and naturally no veneration of the reserved host. Such a practice would be veneration of a created thing, for then only the bread is there. But during the celebration the sacramental union of the body and blood of Christ with the elements exists. From this perspective alone is Luther's discussion of the *consecrated host* to be understood. This finds expression above all in his advisory statements in the cases of Pastors Besserer in Weida and Wolferinus in Eisleben.

On 11 January 1546 Luther expressed himself in a letter to Amsdorf regarding Besserer, who had been imprisoned because he had given a communicant an unconsecrated host in place of a consecrated one that had fallen on the floor (cf. Enders 17:7 n. 2 on No. 3599). Luther opposes his imprisonment but favors his dismissal from office: "Let him go to his Zwinglians!" (Ibid., line 11). "As a mocker of God and of the people he has publicly dared to regard consecrated and unconsecrated hosts as the same thing" [*hostias consecratas ac non consecratas pro eodem habere*] (lines 9f.).

The case of Wolferinus, which happened three years earlier, had to do with the fact that a controversy broke out among the pastors in Eisleben because Wolferinus had put the remaining consecrated elements back with the unconsecrated, referring to the fact that the sacraments are actions [*actiones*], not static facts [*stantes factiones*—things remaining done]. In Luther's first letter to Wolferinus of 4 July 1543, which is also signed by Bugenhagen as one who agreed with Luther's judgment (Enders 15, No. 3285), the Eisleben pastor is urgently admonished to give up this dangerous practice that could lead to Zwinglianism; besides it is against the custom existing in the other churches. The elements that are left over should be consumed by the pastor and the communicants, "so that it will not be necessary to raise such objectionable and dangerous questions about the cessation of the sacramental action" (line 46). This demand corresponds with the repeated advice of the Reformer that what remains [*die "reliquiae"*] should be either consumed or burned. In a second letter of 20 July Luther warns Wolferinus against a misunderstanding of Melanchthon's statement, "There is no sacrament outside of the sacramental action" (Enders 15, No. 3291). Wolferinus is so limiting the sacramental action that he is about to lose the Sacrament. His definition threatens to limit the Real Presence to the consecration, which is indeed the most potent and the principal action in the Sacrament, and would lead to a renewal of the scholastic question, At which of the words does the Presence begin? The action of the Sacrament is not limited to a moment, but actually extends over a period of time. Luther then gives his definition of the *sacramental action* [*actio sacramentalis*]. He expresses it thus, "It starts with the beginning of the Lord's Prayer and lasts until all have communed, the cup has been drunk empty, the hosts have been eaten, and the people have been dismissed and have gone from the altar" (line 34), and he adds: "In this way we will be sure and free from doubts and from the offensive, interminable questions" [*et scandalis quaestionum interminabilium*].

These written answers of Luther correspond to his personal conduct as communicant (on that subject see Hans Preuss, *Luther als Kommunikant: Festschrift für Friedrich Ulmer* [1937], 205ff.) and as celebrant. In many churches in which he celebrated the Lord's Supper there remained for a long time memories of his conduct, e.g., in the Church of Our Lady in Halle during his last journey to Mansfeld. Long afterwards they were still telling of this celebration, one of the last, if not the last of his life.

> The great number of communicants had wearied his aged arms; at one point his quivering hand caused him to spill a little of the consecrated wine on the floor. Luther put the chalice down on the altar, fell to his knees, and sucked up the wine with his mouth so that it should not be trodden under foot, whereupon the whole congregation broke out in sobbing and weeping. (K. Loewe, quoted by K. Anton, *Luther und die Musik* [1928], 59; G. Kawerau offers another report, quoted by Hans Grass, *Die Abendmahlslehre bei Luther und Calvin* [1954], 115–21; Grass's careful treatment of the whole question is emphasized here.)

One may not simply explain these notions of Luther as echoes of his Catholic past. How profoundly he had freed himself from this past we have seen in the discussion of the Sacrifice of the Mass.

It all comes down to the question of whether we are here dealing with private views of Luther and his colleagues and the majority of the Lutheran pastors of the 16th century or whether the doctrine of the consecration that is involved in these views is to be regarded as *doctrine of the Lutheran Church.* For this is what must concern us here above all, not what falls under the heading of liturgy and ritual.

Against the hypothesis that the Formula of Concord confesses this doctrine the Saliger controversy over the Sacrament has repeatedly been cited. In Lübeck and later in Rostock *Saliger* had maintained that the Real Presence is there before the *sumptio*, the receiving of the elements, and he and his followers appeal to Luther. The fact that Saliger was condemned has repeatedly been brought forward to show that according to Lutheran doctrine there is only a Real Presence at the moment of the reception of the consecrated bread and wine. But other factors played a role in his condemnation, above all the way in which he pursued his cause and the expressions that he used (see on that J. Wiggers, *Zeitschrift f. hist. Theol.*, 1848, 613ff.; H. Frank, *Konkordienformel* 3:66f., 146f.; Grass, 111f.). "In this controversy those who were not followers of Saliger, even those who opposed him, did not maintain a Real Presence only in the reception. Wigand shows in his expert opinion, after he has set aside the case, that if the sacramental action is interrupted and there is no reception, there is a Presence before the eating and drinking" (Grass, 111).

In the decision, the Wismar Recess written by Chytraeus, one of the authors of the Formula of Concord, which was partially incorporated into the Solid Declaration [VII, 83-85; *Bekenntnisschriften*, 1000 n. 4], papistic expressions that let the Sacrament exist beyond its use [*extra usum*] are forbidden, but the teaching is also specifically rejected "that the body and blood of Christ are not present in the Lord's Supper until the consecrated bread and wine are touched with the lips or taken into the mouth." Here precisely that view is rejected that later orthodoxy regarded as correct. So it is also not the teaching of the Formula of Concord that the Real Presence is there only in the *sumptio*, in the reception of the elements. This view is explained by the misunderstanding that the *usus*, the use of the Sacrament, is the same thing as the *sumptio*, the reception. Thus the Formula of Concord, making use of the Wismar Recess, decides the question of the effect of the consecration in this way:

> But this blessing or recitation of Christ's words of institution by itself, if the entire action of the Lord's Supper as Christ ordained it is not observed (if, for instance, the blessed bread is not distributed, received, and eaten but is locked up, offered up, or carried about), does not make the sacrament. But the command of Christ, "Do this," which comprehends the whole action or administration of this sacrament (namely, that in a Christian assembly we take bread and wine, consecrate it, distribute it, receive it, eat and drink it, and therewith proclaim the Lord's death), must be kept integrally and inviolately, just as St. Paul sets the whole action of the breaking of bread, or of the distribution and reception before our eyes in 1 Cor. 10:16.
>
> To maintain this true Christian doctrine concerning the Holy Supper and to obviate and eliminate many kinds of idolatrous misuse and perversion of this testament, the following useful *rule* and norm has been derived from the words of institution: Nothing has the character of a sacrament apart from the use instituted by Christ, or apart from the divinely instituted action [*Nihil habet rationem sacramenti extra usum a Christo institutum oder extra actionem divinitus institutam*]. (SD VII 83–85; Müller, 665)

The definition of *usus* as *actio* is then repeated:

> In this context "use" or "action" is . . . the entire external and visible action of the Supper as ordained by Christ: the consecration or words of institution, the distribution and reception, or the oral eating." (SD VII 86)

The reception [*sumptio*] is therefore only a part of the use [*usus*]. The teaching developed here by the Formula of Concord matches exactly the one that we found in Luther. For him also the *usus* is the entire *actio*, and the Real Presence, effected by Christ's Word in the consecration, is bound up in the whole *actio* and can therefore not be restricted to the moment of reception. The consecrated bread is the body of Christ also when it lies on the altar or when the pastor holds it in his hand. This is the Lutheran view.

This view certainly does not allow one thing that the Roman teaching knows: the precise *designation of the moment* at which the Real Presence begins and the moment when it *ceases*. We have observed that Luther in one place takes into account that the Lord's Prayer, which precedes the Words of Institution, belongs to the *actio* that is attended by the Real Presence. When we say that the consecration brings about the Real Presence, we are not making a statement about what Roman theology identifies as the moment of consecration. When we say that after the celebration the consecrated bread is no longer the body of Christ, that is not a statement about the moment when the sacramental union ceases, corresponding to the Roman teaching that the Real Presence ceases when the forms decay.

The designation of these moments was the work of scholastic theology, above all of Thomas. But even Thomas could not give a Scriptural basis for it. He simply concludes from the use of the present tense *est* in the statement, "Hoc est corpus meum," that the effect of the consecration takes place at the moment in which the statement has been fully spoken. The same applies to the words about the cup—while his doctrine of concomitance allows him to assume a presence of the blood together with the body *ex reali concomitantia* (*S. th.* 3, q. 78, art. 6.). But this is only a rational argument. Until the middle of the fourth century the early church never knew anything of a "moment of consecration." It turns up in Cyril of Jerusalem and in Serapion (Egypt) and in the West for the first time in Ambrose (cf. Gregory Dix, *The Shape of the Liturgy* [1947], 240). But to this day the Eastern Church has not arrived at complete clarity about the "moment of consecration" (Words of Institution or epiclesis), while the influences of Latin scholasticism, from which the question was posed to the Eastern Church, are fading. Influence of the Scholastic tradition was also involved when Lutheran theologians sought to designate the moment when the Real Presence begins and the moment when it ends. Here lies the theological error of Saliger, and Chytraeus was absolutely right when he said in his criticism that for the devout heart it is enough to know from the Words of Institution that the body and blood are given to us, and it is useless to argue about the bread on the paten or the bread that is left over (cf. the Latin wording from Wiggers in Grass, 112). The same thing must also be said to the later orthodox theologians, who for logical considerations denied a duration of the Real Presence and confined it to the *moment* of the reception, like Aegidius Hunnius (quoted by F. Pieper, *Christian Dogmatics* 3:373 n. 118, from C. F. W. Walther, *Pastorale*, 175), who tried to show the logical impossibility of a duration of the Real Presence that begins with the consecration. He points to the hypothetical case of a celebration of the Lord's Supper that is interrupted by fire breaking out after the consecration but before the reception. To that we can only say that here exactly the same mistake is made as in Scholasticism. One tries to answer questions that Holy Scripture neither knows nor answers and that therefore the church also cannot answer with rational efforts. We cannot determine the moment of the beginning and the end of the real presence of Christ's body and blood in the Sacrament of the Altar with watch in hand, just as we cannot fix temporally the presence of Christ when two or three are gathered together in His name and therefore the promise of Matt. 18:20 is fulfilled for them. We may never forget that the presence of Christ, His divine and human nature, is always an eschatological miracle in which time and eternity meet.

7.

The Lutheran doctrine of the consecration assumes that every celebration of the Lord's Supper is an unfathomable miracle, just as the first Lord's Supper was not, as the Reformed Church supposes, a parabolic action but also a miracle. Every Lord's Supper that we celebrate is a miracle, no less than the miracles that Jesus did during His days on earth. The same is true, although in another way, of Baptism. As the preaching of the Lord was accompanied by His signs and wonders, so the proclamation of His church is accompanied by the sacraments. And as the deeds of Jesus were the dawn of the coming redemption (Luke 4:18ff.; Matt. 11:4ff.), so in Baptism and in the Lord's Supper we are already given what belongs to the coming world. As often as the church gathers around the table of the Lord it is already the "day of the Lord," i.e., the day of the Messiah (cf. Amos 5:18), the day of His return. This is the original meaning of Sunday as the "day of the Lord," on which John (Rev. 1:9ff.) in the Spirit could participate in the heavenly divine service, while the churches of Asia were gathered for the Lord's Supper (cf. 3:20). Sunday is an anticipation of the parousia. It is this because on that day the Lord comes to His church in the Word and in the Sacrament of the Altar. For this reason the church greets Him before the consecration with "Blessed is he who comes in the name of the Lord. Hosanna in the highest." The old Lutheran Church of the 16th and 17th centuries still celebrated the divine service in this sense, which Article 24 of the Augsburg Confession defends with the words: "We are unjustly accused of having abolished the Mass. Without boasting, it is manifest that the Mass is observed among us with greater devotion and more earnestness than among our opponents." This honor is long past, since late orthodoxy neglected the liturgical instruction of the people, Pietism destroyed the Lutheran concept of sacrament, and rationalism nullified faith in miracles.

Will the Lutheran Church recover the divine service to which its Confession bears witness? It cannot be a matter of repristinating an unrepeatable past but only of understanding anew the teaching of the Holy Scriptures about the Sacrament of the Altar as confessed in the Confession. Everything else will come of itself. It is an experience of the history of Lutheranism in the 19th century that generally, wherever Luther's doctrine of the Real Presence is again understood and believed, hunger for the Sacrament of the Altar wakens afresh, and the liturgy is renewed. We see beginnings of such an experience even today. No liturgical movement can help our church unless it is inspired with Luther's profound understanding of the consecration. In the consecration Jesus Christ is speaking and no one else. He speaks the Word of divine omnipotence: "This is My body," "This is My blood," and of divine love: "Given and shed for you for the forgiveness of sins." And this Word creates what it says, the true presence of His body and blood and the forgiveness of sins. So both forms in which the Gospel appears meet in the consecration, the spoken and the acted Gospel, the Word and the Sacrament. In this sense the consecration is the Gospel itself.

These pages have been written while in Germany the great vital questions for the Lutheran Church are considered in the convention of the Lutheran World Federation in Hannover and in smaller conferences. Whatever the outcome of these meetings may be, let us never forget, esteemed brothers, that the decision about the future of our church and the preservation of the Lutheran Confessions is made in the individual congregation. For there, in the church at a particular place, stands the altar around which the church gathers.

Sanctorum Communio

1974

(Published as chapter 1 of Hermann Sasse, *Corpus Christi: Ein Beitrag zum Problem der Abendmahlskonkordie*, ed. Friedrich Wilhelm Hopf [Erlangen: Verlag der Ev.-Luth. Mission, 1979], 13–29.)

In the old World Conference on Faith and Order, which is not identical with the Commission on Faith and Order of the World Council of Churches, the healthy rule applied that all important documents had to be published not only in the three languages used at the conference but also in Latin and Greek. As long as this rule was observed, the lack of clarity and the ambiguity that unfortunately was often desired were avoided, ambiguity that infuses modern ecumenical documents.

What did it mean for Christendom that the confessional documents of the 16th and 17th centuries, right up to the Westminster Confession, were presented in Latin and that the theologians of all denominations had the opportunity of engaging in genuine dialog with one another, an opportunity of which they made ample use? Today English seems about to become the ecclesiastical language of the Western world; even the *Osservatore Romano* has to have an English edition. Now English certainly belongs among the classical languages of Christendom—one need only think of the English Bible, of Cranmer's liturgical texts, and of the wonderful language of John Henry Newman—but modern English is too noncommittal, too indefinite for dogmatic formulations. Added to this is the dreadful inclination of modern theology to express its thoughts in ever newer terminology. Certainly, the church must and therefore theology may develop new terms when the old terms are no longer understood or are no longer adequate. Classical examples of this are the *homoousios* of the Nicene Creed and the struggle over terminology for the trinitarian and christological dogmas (*ousia, hypostasis, essen-*

tia, substantia, prosōpon, persona, physis, natura, and their laboriously formed and often dubious equivalents in Syrian, Coptic, and Armenian).

But a new terminology is only allowed when it serves to bring clarity, not to confuse the concepts or cloud the truth. Otherwise our theology is in danger of becoming what Harnack called the "systematic misuse of a terminology invented for someone's own purpose." This danger is especially great in the area of modern ecumenical theology.

Such a misfortune seems to lie behind the Leuenberg Concord, which has no less a goal than the establishment of church fellowship between the Lutheran, Reformed, and Union churches of Europe. That is in every respect a utopian undertaking, for such a church fellowship is not only impossible, but it is a logical absurdity. It would be conceivable and commendable to seek a new, closer relationship among these churches. Whatever one might call this relationship, the expression *church fellowship* is impossible because it plays a part in the doctrine and in the ecclesiastical law of the Lutheran Church and not only that, but it goes back to the earliest church and is deeply rooted in the New Testament. It is the fellowship that binds within the one, holy, catholic church all believing individuals and their congregations in the oneness of the body of Christ. It is a fellowship of the church, not of the churches, whether one understands churches to mean local congregations or dioceses, each of which is *the* church of Christ, *the* people of God at that respective place (e.g., in Jerusalem, in Corinth, in Ephesus, in Rome).

The Biblical word for this fellowship is *koinonia, communio.* This *koinonia* is distinct from all other fellowships because it is not of human origin and reaches beyond the range of what is earthly and human. This fellowship is not founded on a social contract or on natural religion, as Schleiermacher taught: "The religious self-consciousness, like every essential element *of human nature,* leads necessarily in its development to *fellowship* or communion: a communion which, on the one hand, is variable and fluid, and on the other hand, has definite limits, i.e., is a church" (Friedrich Schleiermacher, *Der christliche Glaube,* ed. Martin Redecker [Berlin, 1960], 1:41 [*Christian Faith* 1:6]; cf. 2:215 where it says that the church comes into being by the coming together of born-again individuals [2:115]). Rather, it originates in the divine means of grace, the Word of God and the sacraments of Christ. "That which we have seen and heard we proclaim also to you, so that you may have *fellowship with us; and our fellowship is with the Father and with His Son Jesus Christ*" (1 John 1:3; cf. vv. 6f.).

The Greek word for this is *koinonia*. Of the first congregation in Jerusalem immediately after Pentecost and the baptism of the 3,000 it says: "They devoted themselves to the apostles' teaching and fellowship, to the breaking of bread and the prayers" (Acts 2:42). Fellowship is founded in Baptism and finds its concrete expression in the Sacrament of the breaking of bread. That corresponds exactly to the usage of Paul: God has called the believers "into the fellowship of His Son, Jesus Christ our Lord." "By *one* Spirit we were all baptized into *one* body . . . and all were made to drink of *one* Spirit" (1 Cor. 1:9; 12:13). The connection with the Lord's Supper becomes quite clear (1 Cor. 10:16f.). The *koinonia* of the body and blood of Christ coincides with the *koinonia* of the church. We shall return to this passage later.

That the fellowship of the church is at the same time the fellowship of Christians with the Father, the Son, and the Holy Spirit is expressed in the apostolic blessing in 2 Cor. 13:13 [14]. The question has been asked whether the *koinonia tou hagiou pneumatos* means a common sharing of the Holy Spirit or the fellowship that is worked by the Spirit. It is of course both. 1 Cor. 12:13 confirms that it is a result of the Spirit. The word is also used for the consequence or confirmation of this fellowship worked by the Spirit. Thus the collection that Paul gathered from his Gentile Christian congregations for the poor saints in Jerusalem is called *koinonia* (Rom. 15:26; 2 Cor. 9:13), just as in Heb. 13:16 *koinonia* means the gifts of love within the congregation in contrast to the *eupoiia*, the alms one gives outside the congregation. If both are designated as *thysia*, the most solemn word for sacrifice, then we may recall that in Acts 2:42 *koinonia* probably means the bringing of the gifts in the divine service. We would then find in this passage, for the first time, the four basic elements of Christian worship: proclamation of the apostolic word, the breaking of bread, the bringing of the gifts or "communion," and the prayers of the believers. One can ask whether that is an accident.

The Biblical idea of koinonia is echoed in the Third Article of the Western baptismal creed: "I believe in the Holy Spirit, the holy catholic church, the communion of saints [*sanctorum communionem*], the forgiveness of sins, the resurrection of the flesh and the life everlasting." The phrase *sanctorum communionem*, the last addition to this creed that grew by steady development, must be understood from its context. It is not, as was thought for a long time and as Luther still understood it, an explanatory apposition to *sanctam ecclesiam catholicam* as a kind of definition of the church. The Roman Creed, in contrast to the Eastern creeds ("God of God, Light of Light, very God of very God"), has no explanatory repetitions, but with every new idea it introduces a new fact.

Sanctorum communio cannot be understood as a "congregation of saints" [*Gemeinde der Heiligen*]. In biblical Greek *koinonia* never means congregation [*congregatio*]. It designates a state of affairs within the church, the congregation of saints [*congregatio sanctorum*]. Within the holy catholic church there is the *communio sanctorum*, in which *sanctorum* can be the genitive either of *sancti*, the holy persons, or of *sancta*, the holy things, therefore meaning participation in the *sancta* as the consecrated [*geheiligten*] things.

If an expression is found in the Creed with a double meaning, then it may also—as in the corresponding case with a word of Holy Scripture—be understood in a double sense. It would then, if one thinks of holy persons, deal with the *koinonia* that exists according to 1 John 1 between the members of the church, something like the Catholic Church understands its doctrine of the fellowship within the church in its three parts: the church militant, the church triumphant, and the church suffering in purgatory. While we as evangelical theologians must oppose the doctrines of purgatory and of the invocation of the saints, which Rome bases on this concept of the *sanctorum communio*, just as certainly we must hold on to the Biblical doctrine of the *koinonia* between the members of the church in the sense of 1 John 1 and may recover it in the *sanctorum communio*. Indeed, the usage of *ecclesia* in Heb. 12:23 for the city of the living God, the heavenly Jerusalem, allows us to go beyond the scope of the temporal church and to understand with the fathers that all saints and righteous persons from the beginning of the world, indeed even the angels and authorities and powers in heaven [*virtutes et potestates supernae*] are included in the concept of the *ecclesia*, just as Niceta of Remesiana did in his explanation of the Creed (Cf. Werner Elert, *Abendmahl und Kirchengemeinschaft in der alten Kirche hauptsächlich des Ostens* [Berlin, 1954], 170f. [*Eucharist and Church Fellowship in the First Four Centuries* (St. Louis, 1966), 209ff.]; Ferdinand Kattenbusch, *Das apostolische Symbol*, vol. 2: *Verbreitung und Bedeutung des Taufsymbols* [Hildesheim, 1962], 930). He calls this church *sanctorum omnium congregatio*, the congregation of all the saints. "In this one church believe that you will reach the communion of saints" [*In hac una ecclesia crede te communionem consecuturum esse sanctorum*]. The fellowship of the saints is then an eschatological treasure in which the members of the church will take

142

part. This church appears on earth in the form of the catholic church with which one must stand in fellowship ("cuius communionem debes firmiter retinere"). Then follows a warning against the false churches [*pseudo-ecclesiae*] of the heretics and schismatics, who no longer belong to that holy church, because they, deceived by demons, believe and live differently than Christ taught and the apostles handed on.

This understanding of *communio sanctorum*, which is based on Augustine's ecclesiology, is not the original one, however, and therefore is also not the only possible meaning of the expression. There is much evidence that it originally meant participation in the *sancta*, the consecrated elements in the Lord's Supper that had become the body and blood of the Lord. This understanding of *sancta* goes back to the liturgies of the Eastern Church, where the communion is introduced with the call: "The holy things for the holy ones" [*Ta hagia tois hagiois*] (Cf. the proofs in Kattenbusch, 927ff.; Elert, 7ff., 171–81 [209–33]). Even though the personal understanding prevailed in the West, the old meaning was never completely forgotten. Hahn reports a text of the Creed in Old Norman French that gives our passage as *la communion des saintes choses* (holy things) and points to a late explanation of the Creed in German, found in Ulm, that has the same understanding of *sanctorum communio* (August Hahn, *Bibliothek der Symbole und Glaubensregeln der alten Kirche*, 3d ed. [Breslau, 1897], 83).

If this understanding is correct, then we would have the reference to the Sacrament of the Altar that has often been missed in the Creed. In any case it is implied in "communion of saints." For the *koinonia* that according to the New Testament exists among the saints, the believers, finds its strongest expression in the fellowship of those who, gathered around the Lord's table, receive His body and blood. "The cup of blessing which we bless, is it not a *koinonia tou haimatos tou Christou?* The bread which we break, is it not a *koinonia tou somatos tou Christou?*" It is not the action of the blessing and breaking that creates the fellowship but the content of the cup and the bread: "Because there is *one* bread, we who are many are *one* body, for we all partake of the *one* bread." The Greek word for "partake" is *metechomen*, which in the Vulgate is suitably translated with *participamus*, while *koinonia tou somatos tou Christou* is rendered *participatio corporis Domini*, and *koinonia* in verse 16 is rendered *communicatio*. The passage shows how closely the idea of the church as the body of Christ goes together with the concept of the sacramental body in the Lord's Supper. It has been justifiably supposed that Paul derived the idea, unique to him, of the church as the body of Christ from the Lord's Supper. In any case 1 Cor. 10:16f. shows that both meanings of *sanctorum communio* have their root in the expression *koinonia tou somatos tou Christou*. We shall have to examine later how the connection between the *corpus Christi mysticum* and the *corpus sacramentale* is to be determined.

If these observations are correct, then one will no longer be able to say that the understanding of the Lord's Supper is not one of the articles of the faith, as the Reformed have unrelentingly emphasized since Zwingli and Oecolampadius. Luther protested against this from the beginning, above all against the Strasburgers and especially Bucer. The latter always pleaded that both Luther's and Zwingli's understanding of the Lord's Supper had their rightful place in the church and should be tolerated. At the end of the Marburg Colloquy when Bucer with great and honest pathos exhorted both parties to have such tolerance, he got to hear the catastrophic words from Luther: "You have a different spirit." For Luther the doctrine of the Lord's Supper was binding dogma of the church, although he did not find it in the Creed. The Nicene Creed has no counterpart to *sanctorum communio*, but it does count Baptism as an article of faith: "I confess one Baptism for the remission of sins." What is to be believed and confessed is that Baptism gives the forgiveness of sins. That prompts the question whether perhaps the *remissionem peccatorum* in the Apostles' Creed refers to Baptism. It has often been understood in this way, e.g., in a formula in the Gallic church: "through Holy Baptism, the forgiveness of sins" [*per baptismum sanctum remissionem peccatorum*] (Hahn, 77). A creed in a manuscript of the eighth and ninth centuries reads, "remission of sins either through Baptism or through Penance" [*remissionem peccatorum sive per baptisma, sive per poenitentiam*] (Ibid., 99).

If one wants to judge these variants and the uncertainty that they reveal correctly, one must give thought to the fact that the "Third" Article has also remained a problem in the Eastern Church. At Nicaea they were content with the words "and in the Holy Spirit." The original Nicene Creed is really a binitarian creed. Only in the great debates over the meaning of the *homoousios* did Athanasius reach the conclusion that the *homoousios* of the Son is not intelligible without the *homoousios* of the Holy Spirit. At the synod of Alexandria in 362 an agreement was reached with the Cappadocians and their doctrine that Father, Son, and Holy Spirit are of the *same* essence (*homoios kat' ousian* = *homoousios*), not of *one* essence, which *homoousios* originally meant. It was the great concession made by Athanasius that *homoousios* could be used in both ways, so that to this day the fine distinction exists between the Eastern Church and the West in that there one understands the Trinity as three-in-one [*Dreieinigkeit*], here as threefold [*Dreifaltigkeit*]. The result of all this lies before us in the Constantinopolitan Creed of 381, our "Nicene Creed." When the Council of Chalcedon accepted both texts as equally valid and recognized the synod of 381 as "ecumenical," the Creed was brought to completion. Yet even today it bears the character of something unfinished. A clear testimony of the Spirit as *homoousios* is lacking. Only the West has made up for the omission in the *filioque* of the Nicene Creed and in the Athanasian Creed. In a version of the Creed in the Old Irish Church we read: "Credo in Spiritum sanctum, deum omnipotentem, habentem substantiam cum patre et filio; sanctam ecclesiam, abremissa (*abremissa*, the Late Latin form for *abremissio*—cf. *missa* for *missio*, *collecta* for *collectio*—are found in other texts; note the sequence: the Sacrament of Baptism precedes the Eucharist) peccatorum, sanctorum communionem . . ." (Hahn, 84f.). It would lead us too far afield to quote here further examples from the Middle Ages of how *communio* and *remissio* are used with reference to the sacraments.

And where else but in the Third Article would there be room for a doctrine of the sacraments? It is not only the article of faith about the church that suggests this connection, but the whole article as such, for the Holy Spirit is pertinent to the "last things." He is indeed eternal God, from everlasting to everlasting. As such He shares in the creation and preservation of the world. To Him belongs the kingdom of nature as well as the kingdom of grace. He gives man life (Job 32:8), joy (Ps. 51:14), and wisdom and leads him on a level path (Ps. 143:10). The extraordinary powers of the warrior, the special gifts of the artist and of the ruler, and above all the gift of prophecy are His work. But above all, the fulfillment of the end time will bring a full measure of the Spirit for the whole people of God (Is. 44:3; Joel 3:1f.). Even the resurrection of the dead is the work of the Holy Spirit (Ezek. 37). With the resurrection of Christ as the firstborn from the dead, the resurrection of all the dead has begun (1 Cor. 15:20ff). Since then it is "the last hour" (1 John 2:18). Now at the end of the world the Son of God has indeed appeared (Heb. 1:2). Now the prophecy of Joel about the outpouring of the Spirit of God on the whole people of God is fulfilled. Now the Spirit no longer rests on individual people, on kings and prophets, but on the whole people of God in the whole church. One can speak of church in a general sense. Church was the whole people of God, all saints and believers from the beginning of the world. But the church of Christ, church in the full sense, has only existed since Easter and Pentecost.

And to the church belong the sacraments or—in order to avoid the ambiguous and so often misused word of ecclesiastical Latin—Baptism, absolution, and the Lord's Supper. Whatever one may want to call these things, whether one speaks of sacraments with the Latin church or of mysteries with the Eastern church, or whether one simply designates them collectively with a term like "means of grace," they all have one thing in common: they have an eschatological significance. In them the future redemption is already present. They denote not only a divine, heavenly reality, but they give us a share in it already now. The forgiveness of sins that we receive in Baptism and absolution is the anticipation of the acquittal of the Last Judgment. Our death and our resurrection to eternal life have already begun in our baptism (Rom. 6:3ff.). In Holy Communion Christ comes already now and gives us a share in the "messianic" banquet in heaven. It would have been better to understand the sacraments in this way as anticipation of the redemption of the end time instead of forcing them into the scheme of the sign theory. Augustine gave it its start. The commanding authority that he won in the West bequeathed this scheme to all Western churches. Thus, to give only one example, in *De civ. Dei* (10, 5) he calls the visible sacrifice the "sacrament or sacred sign of an invisible sacrifice" [*invisibilis sacrificii sacramentum id est sacrum signum*]. Since then Medieval theology understood sacrament as sign. In the first edition of his *Loci* even Melanchthon dealt with the sacraments under the heading "On Signs." Johann Gerhard is the first one for whom sacrament is no longer "in the category of signs" [*in genere signi*] (Thomas Aquinas, *Summa theologica* 3, q. 60, art. 1) but "in the category of action" [*in genere actionis*]. How dangerous the sign theory is may be seen from Augustine's thought that sacraments belong to the essence of every religion, the true as well as the false. How much distress of unnecessary controversy, how many misunderstandings and false teachings Christendom would have been spared if from the beginning one would have remained with what Holy Scripture teaches about Baptism, the Lord's Supper, and absolution instead of forcing these holy actions onto the Procrustean bed of Neoplatonic philosophy.

But in the fourth century there was no longer anyone able to do that. By then the Christian faith had risen into the upper levels of society, and so had gotten into the hands of those whose thought was shaped by late antiquity and by the heathen religiosity of a certain philosophy. What Augustine says of his own conversion applies much the same to all the heathen who found the way to Christ: "Late have I loved you." Late, in many cases much too late, did they encounter the Gospel. Thus the great Alexandrians, also the Biblical theologian Origen, read it with late Greek eyes. It is a proof of the indestructible vitality of the divine Word that it even survived this.

The East did not develop a doctrine of the sacraments in the Augustinian-Western sense, if only because it did not know the word *sacrament*. Instead, the Eastern Church spoke of mysteries. That "sacrament" is the same thing as "mystery" was not completely forgotten in the West. Hugo of St. Victor still treated his dogmatics under the title "On the sacraments" and accordingly spoke of the sacrament of the Trinity, etc. The original difference in meaning between the Latin and the Greek word consists of the fact that *sacramentum* (from *sacer, sacrare*) looks at the action of man, at his praying, sacrifice, etc. Thus in later Latin *sacra* becomes the designation of the cultus. The governor of Carthage warned the martyrs of Scilli not to say anything evil *de sacris nostris*, that is, about the heathen cultus of the state (*Passio Sanctorum Scillitanorum* 5, Rudolf Knopf, *Märtyrer-Akten*, 3d ed., ed. G. Krüger [Giessen, 1929], 29f. [Hardy, *Faithful Witnesses*, 29]). *Sacramentum* appears originally to have meant "dedication," later also the oath of loyalty made by recruits, a meaning that also acquired significance for Zwingli. *Mysterium*, on the other hand, designates the divine secret and what this secret suggests and imparts. In medieval Latin the words are used without distinction—probably under the influence of the Vulgate—as in the usage of modern German Catholics one can still speak of receiving communion as receiving the holy mysteries. (The best discussion of the language problem is presented in the commentary of the German edition of Thomas: *Thomas von Aquin: Vollständige, ungekürzte deutsch-lateinische Ausgabe der Summa Theologica*, ed. Katholischer Akademikerverband [Salzburg and Leipzig, 1938], 30:385ff.)

We have commented on the problem of the language history because it casts a bright light on the history of Eucharistic teachings. The uncertainty of the theological doctrines is partially a result of the ambiguity of the terminology. In what matters here, however, there is no difference between East and West. In "sacrament" as in "mystery" the thing that is meant by the body of Christ is the same. It is the body that was born of His mother Mary, that died on the cross, that was buried, rose from the dead, ascended into heaven, and is sitting at the right hand of the Father (cf. the medieval hymn "O Lord, We Praise You" [*Gott sei gelobet und gebenedeiet*], whose thoughts ring through countless liturgies of East and West and that our church still sings in many languages with the second and third stanzas added by Luther).

This and nothing else is the church's dogma of the Lord's Supper. It stands behind the *sanctorum communionem*. There are two reasons why it is not expressed in an explicit article of faith. First, there was no church or heresy that had challenged it. And second, it is there in all liturgies of Christian antiquity. There probably have been individual theologians who have questioned or challenged it—what have theologians not challenged? But there is no liturgy of the Lord's Supper that did not contain it or take it for granted. The New Testament already contains the first traces of a Christian liturgy of the Lord's Supper. The four accounts of the institution already bear clear characteristics of liturgical texts. The oldest fragment, which goes back to the Aramaic beginning of the church, is the "Marana tha" (1 Cor. 16:22). It is contained, still in its original Aramaic form, in the *Didache* (10. 6), while it appears at the end of Revelation (22:20) in Greek translation: *erchou Kyrie Jesu* (Come, Lord Jesus). It could be that behind it stands a Jewish prayer for the coming of the Messiah. This is suggested by the custom that has been preserved among Jews and Christians in the East down to our own day of leaving a place "for the Messiah" empty at solemn meals. That in Paul as well as in John (cf. also *Did.* 10) the *charis* formula ("The grace of the Lord Jesus Christ . . .") follows, with which the Eucharist still begins in the Eastern Church today, could be an indication of such a connection.

In a much later form, behind which a Greek text could stand, such a prayer for the coming of Jesus to his congregation celebrating the Eucharist is found in the Mozarabic liturgy as an introduction to the Eucharistic prayer: "Come, come, Jesus, good Priest, in the midst of us, just as You were in the midst of Your disciples. Consecrate this offering so that we may eat the consecrated things by the hand of Your holy angel, O holy Lord and everlasting Redeemer." Then came the Words of Institution and the Postpridie, which begins with the words: "Lord Jesus Christ, consecrate this living sacrifice by the light of [Your] coming." The Lord is asked to be in the midst of His congregation, as He was once in the midst of His disciples at the Last Supper, and to do what He did then, namely, bless the gifts put before Him. This "blessing" (*hagiazein, sanctificare*) is clearly more than the blessing of ordinary food with the word of God and prayer according to 1 Tim. 4:5. Here *sanctificare* means what we would call "consecrate," as in the prayer to the *sanctificator* in the Roman Offertory. (It appears that the "Veni sanctificator, omnipotens aeterne Deus, et benedic hoc sacrificium . . ." is a remnant of an old epiclesis to the Spirit. Mozarabic and Gallic forms add "Spirit" or "Paraclete." "Sanctificator" is a title of the Holy Spirit.) As it is the Holy Spirit in the East who descends in the *epiphoitesis* on the offered gifts and makes them the body and blood of the Lord, so here Jesus is the consecrator. He does the same thing that He did at the institution: He speaks the Words of Institution and thereby consecrates the elements. That is the meaning of this old liturgy.

What makes the Sacrament a *sacramentum*, the mystery a *mysterion* is the fact that bread and wine become the body and blood of Christ. This and nothing else is the church's dogma of the Lord's Supper. The body and blood of the Lord are therefore the holy things [*sancta*] that are given to the communicants in order to make them the holy ones [*sancti*] and thereby bind them to the unity and fellowship of Christ's body. It is this thought of unity, which finds its perfect expression in Jesus' "high-priestly prayer" (John 17), that Hoskyns (Edwin Hoskyns, *The Fourth Gospel*, ed. F. N. Davey [London, 1947], 494ff.) rightly calls the "consecration prayer," in which Jesus consecrates Himself as the sacrifice and presents His disciples and the church of all ages to the Father: ". . . that they may all be one; even as Thou, Father, art in Me, and I in Thee, that they also may be in us. . . . I in them and Thou in Me, that they may become perfectly one . . ." [vv. 21, 23]. That is the perfect communion of saints, *sanctorum communio* in the dual meaning of the term.

As in John 17 the gaze of our praying Lord goes from this world to that of the future ("Father, I desire that they also, whom Thou hast given Me, may be with Me where I am, to behold My glory" [v. 24]), so the gaze upward to heaven belongs to the essence of the Eucharistic liturgy: *Elevatis oculis*. In most liturgies of the East and West the Son speaks the Words of Institution to God His almighty Father, just as in John 17:1 the upward look introduces the great prayer. That heaven and earth become one, as it were, in the Eucharist is one of the fundamental thoughts in the great liturgical chapter, Rev. 4. Erik Peterson has shown (*Das Buch von den Engeln: Stellung und Bedeutung der heiligen Engel im Kultus* [Leipzig, 1935], 323ff.) how the parallels there go right down to the details. Thus the Sanctus belongs to the temporal as well as the heavenly divine service. As Isaiah heard it in the vision of his call from the mouth of the seraphim surrounding the throne of

God, so it rings in its New Testament form in Rev. 4:8 (". . . who was and is and is to come"). The Sanctus is the angels' song of praise before the face of God "in never silent theologies" (thus the Greek liturgies). It is sung in the presence of God. Isaiah heard it in the temple at Jerusalem, the earthly dwelling place of the glory [*kabod, doxa*] of Yahweh (cf. Ps. 26:8). John heard it in the heavenly sanctuary on the Lord's Day while the church on earth was celebrating the Sacrament. Thus its worship and its Sanctus—and this applies to all the church's liturgies—encompass heaven and earth at the same time. The Trisagion now refers to the Triune God. The Lord whose praise is sung is He who was and who is and who is to come. According to John 12:41 it was indeed Christ's glory that the prophet saw. How inseparably faith in the almighty Father and the confession of the complete divinity of Christ are connected is shown by a passage like Rev. 5:13: "To Him who sits upon the throne and to the Lamb be blessing and honor and glory and might forever and ever!" to which 4:11 ("Worthy art Thou, our Lord and God") and 5:12 ("Worthy is the Lamb") may be compared.

The Sanctus of Isaiah 6 has appeared in the Christian divine service since the second Christian century. Perhaps the example of the synagogue somehow helped to bring that about. (The best discussion of the problem of the Jewish kiddush and the Trisagion in their relationship to the Sanctus of the church is offered by Josef Andreas Jungmann, S.J., *Missarum Sollemnia: Eine genetische Erklärung der römischen Messe*, 4th ed. [Freiburg, 1958], 2:166.) 1 Clement 34:6f. shows that it was used in the earliest Roman congregation in connection with Dan. 7:10:

> Ten thousand times ten thousand stood by Him and thousands of thousands served Him and cried out: "Holy, holy, holy is the Lord of hosts; the whole creation is full of His glory." And we also, gathered with one accord and devoutly, would cry to Him emphatically as with one mouth, that we may share in His great and glorious promises. For the Scripture says, "No eye has seen and no ear has heard and it has not entered man's heart what the Lord has prepared for those who wait for Him.

That this does not yet belong to the Eucharistic liturgy is shown by the fact that there is still no mention of an identification of the Lord with Jesus Christ, and no coming of the Lord is hinted at or prayed for. The gulf between heaven and earth still exists; the Hosanna, with which one greets Him who comes (Rev. 4:8), is still missing. The text of 1 Clement 34 is older than the great liturgical chapter, Rev. 4. From this we do not say, of course, that the earliest Roman church did not know the Real Presence. The letter of Ignatius to the Romans (7:3) contains one of the passages in which the bishop and martyr speaks of the flesh and blood of Christ, clearly reminiscent of John 6:53: "God's bread is what I desire, that is the flesh of Jesus Christ, who (is descended) from the seed of David; and for drink I desire His blood, which is an imperishable love." Without the realistic understanding, the constant Jewish-heathen accusation of ritual murder and cannibalism in the Christian Agape would probably also be incomprehensible.

It would lead us too far afield if we now wanted to go further into the history of the Eucharistic liturgy, in which the dogma of the Lord's Supper found its fullest expression. One must let oneself be influenced by the stirring prayers of the earthly church, the doxologies in which the church on earth becomes one with the church in heaven, and the awe-inspiring songs in so many languages in order to understand that in this Sacrament beats the heart of the church. Who can deny that this history is also the history of serious errors, even of occasional reversion to heathenism? Who can deny that again and again reforms were necessary, in which case a necessary reformation often degenerated into an unnecessary revolution? That happened not only in the 16th century, but even in our age when liturgical knowledge and art have blossomed as never before, as the Second Vatican Council carried out a reform of the Roman Mass, in which no less a man than St. Zwingli seems to have served as its godfather. But by and large the history of the Eucharistic liturgy was indeed the real heart of church history.

Today as always people ask, What does the church actually do? It prays. The praying church [*ecclesia orans*] is one of the constantly recurring themes of early Christian art. The church prays. Thus it was at the beginning. "All these with one accord devoted themselves to prayer" it says of the first believers after Christ's ascension (Acts 1:14). "They devoted themselves to the apostles' teaching and fellowship, to the breaking of bread and the prayers" it says of the church at Pentecost [2:42]. "Day by day, attending the temple together and breaking bread in their homes, they [were] . . . praising God and having favor with all the people" (v. 46).

They founded no mission society, organized no city mission, wrote no books on "dynamic evangelism." Instead, they celebrated the Sacrament and prayed continually. "And the Lord added to their number day by day those who were being saved" (2:47). And they went on praying. The leader of the apostles was imprisoned, "but earnest prayer for him was made to God by the church" until the chains fell from his hands and the door of the prison swung open (12:5ff.). And so it went on.

What does the church do? What could it do in those last years of Jerusalem to solve the problem of Palestine, which the world's political powers have been trying in vain for centuries to do? What could the church do to stop the ruin of the Roman Empire and of the inestimable treasures of ancient culture? Instead of holding world conferences and having endless debates about the boundaries between church and culture, it went on praying without ceasing and sang the Te Deum on the debris of a world that was coming to an end. None of its prayers were in vain. They rose to heaven, even though they died away on earth. Only fragments have been preserved for us of what is left of the great liturgical books of the early church in the languages of the East. Only remnants have been preserved for us and are still in use in the small fragments of early Christendom that have survived the storm of Islam. The devotional literature of the last century pales before the fervor, the brilliance, the graphic power and beauty, the wonderful language of what is still available to us of these treasures in Greek and Latin. There is no human desire that would be too small or too great to find a stirring expression in these prayers. And always it is the altar before which these prayers are uttered; it is the *Maranatha*, the prayer for the coming of the Lord in the Sacrament as the anticipation of His Parousia; it is the Sanctus and the Eucharistic prayers with the Words of Institution of the Lord's Supper that are framed by these prayers. One can perhaps understand the belief in the Real Presence completely only when one has understood these prayers. Here God is present, the Triune God, the Father, the Son, and the Holy Spirit. Here all philosophy comes to an end. Here is what the early church calls "theology," the praise of God in the sense that John did it, to whom the church has given the nickname "theologian" [*theologos*]. This is no theology of the mysteries in the sense of heathen or semi-heathen mysticism. It is certainly not "the divine," a supernatural reality that we call divine and that is idle talk about our own divinity, that is presented here. Christ does not just appear as a man like an angel in the Old Testament or an avatar in Hinduism, like Krishna in the Bhagavad-Gita, a god in a human form, which He sets aside again in order to return to the divine world of the spirit. The risen and ascended One also remains the Incarnate, as He remains the Crucified. *Quod semel assumpsit, numquam deposuit—* what He once took up, He has never laid aside, as we theologians say.

152

This truth of the real incarnation finds its full expression in the fact that He gives us His true body and His true blood to eat and to drink, so that the *koinonia*, the fellowship that we have with Him in the Sacrament, is not merely something "purely spiritual." That the Lutheran Church has accepted this teaching of the Greek fathers emerges already from the references that the Apology to Article 10 of the Augsburg Confession quotes: "Therefore we must consider that Christ is in us, not only according to the habit which we understand as love, but also by a natural participation" (Ap X 3; cf. the whole text with the quotations from Theophylact and Cyril of Alexandria and further literature in *Bekenntnisschriften*, 248).

We cannot go into the liturgy as a source for the dogma of the Lord's Supper here any further. Only one point still needs a brief reflection: the reception of Communion. The prefatory prayers, the formula of distribution, and the response of the communicants are an unambiguous witness to the belief in the Real Presence. A few examples must suffice. In the Liturgy of St. Mark the priest says at the communion of the clergy: "Behold, it is consecrated and consummated and has become the body and blood of our Lord, God and Savior and what is holy [*das Heilige*] is given to the holy ones [*den Heiligen*]" (F. E. Brightman, *Liturgies Eastern and Western* [Oxford, 1896], 138–39). Since the earliest time the formula of distribution has rung out: *soma Christou*, "the body of Christ" (*Kirchenordnung Hippolyts*, Edgar Hennecke, Neutestamentliche Apokryphen, 2d ed. [Tübingen, 1924], 580. Hugo Duensing, *Der Aethiopische Text der Kirchenordnung des Hippolyt* [Göttingen, 1946], 61. *Apost. Const.* 8. 13), "the holy body of our Lord God and Savior," "the precious blood . . ." (The Liturgy of St. Mark, Brightman, 140). The formula finds itself under Eastern influence also in the Latin liturgies (witnessed by Augustine in Africa; in a very similar form in the Mozarabic liturgy as well as in Milan [Ambrose, *De mysteriis* 9. 54, MPL 16:424; *De sacramentis* 4. 5. 25, MPL 16:464; cf. Jungmann, 2:481 n. 102]). The response of the communicant is in every case "Amen." Ambrose explains the profound seriousness of this Amen: "That is true; I believe it" (Ambrose, *De sacramentis* 4. 5. 25, MPL 16:464). In many liturgies of the East the Words of Institution, which were still spoken aloud, were originally also confirmed by the Amen of the congregation. (Cf. Jungmann, 2:482. It also happened that the first part of the *verba testamenti* was spoken softly and only the second part was said aloud. Then the Amen followed the second part. See the fragment of an old southern Italian liturgy in C. A. Swainsow, *The Greek Liturgies* [Cambridge, 1884], 198.)

How much in earnest the church was about this Amen is shown by the Liturgy of Chrysostom in the confession that preceded the reception of Communion. It was spoken by every single one, by the priest before his own Communion, then by the deacon when he received Communion from the hands of the priest, then by all the communicants together. It begins with the words "I believe and I confess" and then contains the sentence: "I believe that this is truly Your spotless body and that this is truly Your precious blood." An especially strong confession of this sort is found in a text of the liturgy of the Coptic Jacobites, which Brightman gives in English translation:

> This is in truth the body and blood of Immanuel, our God, Amen. I believe, I believe, I believe and I confess to my last breath that this is the life-giving flesh, which Your only begotten Son, our Lord and our God and our Savior Jesus Christ, took from the lady of us all, the holy mother of God, and united with His divinity without mixture, without transformation, and without change. After He had made the good confession before Pontius Pilate, He gave it also for us of His own will on the holy tree of the cross. I believe truly that His divinity was not separated from His humanity for even one moment or instant. It was given for us that it might be for the salvation, for the forgiveness of sins, and for the eternal life of those who receive it. I believe that this is truly so. Amen.

Whereupon the deacon spoke: "Amen, amen, amen. I believe, I believe, I believe that it is truly so" (Brightman, 185).

This text from an old Monophysite church shows the anti-Chalcedonian position of this church. But for the dogma of the Lord's Supper that makes no difference. It is a most remarkable fact that the Orthodox, the Monophysites, and the Nestorians, with all their other dogmatic differences, show no difference in the doctrine of the Lord's Supper of their liturgies. The Mass as it was celebrated in the Nestorian churches of the Persian Empire is essentially the same as that of the Orthodox Church of the empire.

How seriously the East Syrian church—which had even spread all the way to South India and so for centuries in the Middle Ages was the most geographically extensive of all churches—took the consecration [*Heiligung*] of the elements is shown by a recently discovered instruction of Theodore of Mopsuestia, the greatest biblical scholar of the Syrian church: "When the priest distributes, he says, 'The body of Christ . . .';

therefore you say after him, 'Amen.' You then reverence after you have received the body with your hands . . . . With great and true love impress it on your eyes and kiss it and then offer your prayers to it as to our Lord Christ, who is near to you" (Hans Lietzmann, *Kleine Schriften*, vol. 3: *Studien zur Liturgie- und Symbolgeschichte und zur Wissenschaftsgeschichte*, ed. Kommission für Spätantike und Religionsgeschichte [Berlin, 1962], 84, no. 36f. This is the Syrian text published by Mingana in 1933, introduced, translated and edited by Lietzmann [*Sitzungsberichte der Berliner Akademie*, 1933; quotation from p. 13/925]).

That is therefore the dogma of the early church concerning the Lord's Supper: Bread and wine in the Lord's Supper after the consecration are the body and blood of the Lord. Nothing more? No, nothing more. There are, of course, questions for which we would like to have an answer. The one thing that the liturgy does say beyond this is that the presence is effected by the prayer for the Holy Spirit, who, by His coming down on the gifts, "changes" them into the body and blood of the Lord. The technical term of the Greek liturgy for this is *metaballein*, in Latin *mutare*. The elements thus become something that they were not before. The early church does not know a definition of this change analogous to the Roman transubstantiation. The Eastern Church first took over this doctrine as *metusiosis* in the Middle Ages under Roman influence, but it never did become binding dogma for the East. That was already impossible because a dogma could only be accepted by the whole church represented by an ecumenical council. None of the seven recognized councils had done this, if one disregards an indirect decision of the Second Council of Nicaea in 787. This synod rejected a decision of an iconoclastic synod of Constantinople (754), which declared that the only permissible images (icons) in the church were the consecrated elements. The Seventh Ecumenical Council thereby confirmed the explanation that had so often been given by the Greek fathers that the bread and the wine before the consecration could be regarded as types [*typos, antitypos*] of the body and blood, but not the consecrated elements, which had actually become the body and blood of the Lord. (Thus John of Damascus says in *De fide orthodoxa* 4. 13: "When some call the bread and the wine images of the body and blood of the Lord, as did Basil Theophorus, they did not believe this to be the case after the consecration but before the consecration. They spoke this way of the offering [what the congregation had brought to the altar]." Cf. Cyril of Jerusalem, *Mystagogica Cathechesis* 1. 7, 5. 6, MPG 33:1071. *Antitypa* is even used in the epiclesis of the Liturgy of Basil. The use of the word does not detract from the realism.)

How this miracle is then conceivable is something the church fathers wondered about just as theologians of all times have done. They set up theological theories about it, but the doctrine of the church remained uninfluenced by them. It is a serious failure of our textbooks on the history of dogma that they scarcely make a distinction between dogma and theological opinion, between the doctrine that the church confesses *magno consensu* and the theological theories that men, more or less pious and more or less learned theologians, set up.

Since Justin and his pupil Irenaeus the miracle of the incarnation has been used for the explanation: As the Word took on flesh, so the bread and wine receive a divine quality and become bearers of the body and blood of Christ through the Eucharistic prayer (Justin, *Apologie* 1. 66, MPG 6:427–30) or through the epiclesis (Irenaeus, *Adversus haereses* 4. 18. 5, MPG 7/1:1027ff.). It is impossible to understand the thoughts that are clothed in the language and thought world of the mysteries individually as "realistic" or "symbolic" in the modern sense. Wherever Neoplatonism has determined the theological thinking, the symbolic-spiritual side may come to the fore, but we must guard against applying the categories of later centuries to Christian antiquity and its theology. It should also give one pause that the later christological schools all take the same liturgy for granted. The great Antiochene, Theodore of Mopsuestia, compares what happened at the coming of the Holy Spirit with Christ's resurrection; the one is as real for him as the other. Just as there were various views in the early church regarding the baptism of children, so there were also various theological opinions about the understanding of the Eucharist. But just as the baptismal liturgy was the same, whether an adult or a child was baptized (the only exception was the Listurian church, which had a special liturgy for the baptism of children) and no one denied the validity of infant baptism, so all received the Eucharist with the same formula of distribution, "The body of Christ . . . the blood of Christ," and they all thereupon with the church of all ages spoke the Amen of faith.

Credo sanctorum communionem. Sancta sanctis. Ta hagia tois hagiois. The whole secret of the Biblical concept of koinonia is contained in these sentences. They bear witness to the fact that the church and the Lord's Supper, church fellowship and altar fellowship, belong inseparably together. Around the Lord's table His congregation gathers in order to become one with Him by receiving His true body and blood.

156

Church fellowship is not founded "on the assembling of born-again individuals in orderly interaction and cooperation" as Pietism thinks and as the "Moravian of a higher order," Schleiermacher, formulated it (*The Christian Faith*, 2:215). It is also not based on the association of philosophical convictions, as the Enlightenment of all ages has supposed.

As the body of Christ, it is a fellowship unique [*sui generis*], which cannot be made intelligible either in psychological or in sociological categories. Even in terms of the history of religions it is without parallels. The "congregation" with which the convert to Buddhism takes "refuge" is nothing like the body of Buddha. Even the sacrifices, cultic meals, and other rites of ancient heathenism, whose similarities to the Christian sacraments were not first noticed by modern historians of religion but already by the ancient enemies of the church, explain basically nothing else than the truth that "every dogma is as old as the world."

Church fellowship is also not what modern "ecumenical" theology— also in those churches that ought to know better—reads into John 17 and Ephesians 4 in order then to proclaim it as the saving Gospel for our time, namely, the wonderful organization that will arise tomorrow when the hundreds of Christian churches and sects that belong to the World Council of Churches embrace with "this kiss for all the world." This kiss would certainly not be "the holy kiss" with which the church of the New Testament began the celebration of the Eucharist but another kind of kiss, of which the New Testament also tells us.

It would be a puzzle how so many sincere Christians of all confessions could fall victim to such an error if we knew nothing of the serious and contagious disease of chiliasm. The unity of the church of which our Lord speaks in John 17, a unity for which there are no earthly parallels and which therefore is definable in no theology, is the rightly understood, i.e., according to the analogy of faith, *ut omnes unum sunt:* "That they may all be one, even as Thou, Father, art in Me, and I in Thee, that they also may be in us, so that the world may believe that Thou hast sent Me" (v. 21). The "world" is naturally not just the sum of all people who would be living on the earth at the time of the final fulfillment of this wish. It means either the whole number of those whom the Father has given to the Son (17:2, 6) or it means the world at its end. According to the New Testament it can not be said that there will ever come a time in the course of world history when unbelief and therewith sin has disappeared from the world of men. Until then the *una sancta* and the *sanctorum communio* remain articles of faith.